"You can certainly enjoy life without ever having played pickleball, but I wouldn't recommend it."

For Jo, my partner before, during and after pickleball.

And to Pat Crowley, the gifted cartoonist, illustrator and friend who helped make my words come alive with his imaginative drawings in this book.

I Dink, Therefore I Am

*Coming to Grips with
My Pickleball Addiction*

Frank Cerabino

I Dink, Therefore I Am --
Coming to Grips with
My Pickleball Addiction

Joining the cult

Maybe you bought this book on your own, or maybe somebody gave it to you along with a new set of paddles and some funny looking plastic balls with lots of holes in them.

Either way, welcome to the club. You've been pickleballed.

Don't be insulted. It isn't necessarily a subtle suggestion that you should lose 10 pounds or take a break from knitting or bread making.

It's just that pickleball has become a thing. There's no sport growing faster in America than pickleball.

And it's not only happening to broken-down old tennis players and people living behind guard gates in communities with names that evoke the French Riviera or the Amalfi Coast, but are actually built on reclaimed swamp land or scorched desert floor.

We are living through a yet-to-crest pickleball wave, you might say, and as somebody who has been swept away, I want to tell you about it. To evangelize even.

I'm sorry. I can't help myself. I keep thinking about you, the new player — or at least the potential new player — who has been browbeaten into cultural recreational compliance.

Sure, maybe it wasn't your idea to get those paddles. (Yes, they're called "paddles" in pickleball. "Rackets" are what tennis players hold.)

And maybe you think you have the kind of limited hand-eye coordination and lack of fast-twitch muscle command that makes court games a challenge.

But it doesn't matter. Trust me on this. Unless you're in an iron lung, you can play this game and enjoy it. And my guess is that within a few years, USA Pickelball will be offering an iron-lung division at tournaments.

It's a very inclusive game, and with more than 4 million people playing it in America, more than 1 percent of the entire population, you're bound to cross paths with three other people at your skill level to round out a fun foursome.

So yes, I'm doing this to encourage you. But I'm not one of those 5.0 superstar players who gets paid to endorse a certain ball or paddle. I don't have a podcast.

And I've never posted a pickleball instructional YouTube video sponsored by Hyland's Leg Cramps tablets.

I'm kind of like you. At least I was until March 2020 when I first became enthralled with pickleball. It was, coincidentally, the year I also turned 65-years-old, making me a card-carrying member of the class of people who get called "sir", by wisenheimers who are in their 50s.

Would a psychiatrist say my headlong tumble into pickleball is the manifestation of my fear of death? I don't know. Probably.

But I would have a question for that psychiatrist.

"Have you ever tried playing pickleball?"

And if the answer is "No," then I'd say this:

"Well, that explains why you would ask such a silly question. Because if you tried pickleball you'd probably say it was the most fun you had standing up."

And then I'd come in for the slam to this pop-up question.

"You'd have to be crazy not to like pickleball," I'd tell that psychiatrist, who might be smart, but probably clueless when it comes to dinking.

Oh, "dinking" is one of those pickleball words. Relax, I explain it in the book, along with a lot of other introductory things that will make your first forays to the pickleball court more enjoyable.

Here's the way I picture it. For reasons previously explained, you ended up with paddles, balls and this book with the expectation that you will find one of America's 8,700 pickleball courts to give it a try.

And so, you put this book on your toilet tank, perhaps the most important book shelf in every home. And over time, these pages will both bolster your courage and give you an idea of the world you are entering.

And then one day, "Fly, little bird, fly!" you burst from the couch — gently, you don't want to blow out a hammy — and onto a pickleball court wearing a pair of shorts you wished were two inches longer. And for the first time in your life, you utter those profound words for all the world to hear:

"Zero, zero, two."

Oh, excuse me, I'm getting verklempt. I'm going to have to pause to dab at the corners of my eyes and blow my nose.

Sorry, I get emotional when thinking about pickleball.

I know. I should know better. It's a game with a silly name, and when you first see it being played in your local park, it may look more like a movie set for *Honey, I Shrunk the Ping-Pong Players*.

But there's more than meets the eye with pickleball. I try to give you a sense of that in this book to validate your decision to get out there.

In that respect, this is less a "how to" book than a "why to" book.

Along the way, I do dispense some playing tips. But like I said, I'm not a pro. I'm mired in blissful mediocrity.

And I'd like to clue you into its pleasures.

I'm confident I can get you to feel good about that new set of paddles waiting to be used. And to discover, if you're like me, that pickleball can become a habit that you're not willing to shake.

So, congratulations. You're on the precipice of joining the cult.

Game on.

1

The Pickleball Evangelist

I remember the day it dawned on me that I had a problem.

Up until then, I had managed to live 65 years of my life without falling to the usual addictions: YouTube pet videos, reality TV shows based on tropical islands, or food samples at Costco.

If I had a motto, it would be something along the lines of, "Everything in moderation."

But there I was, on a weekday afternoon when I was allegedly still at work. Instead, I was sitting in a public park next to a children's playground, being anything but moderate.

I was alone, and looking longingly at every car that entered the parking lot. I tried not to look needy, but I think my desperation, as evidenced by my tapping foot, was showing.

Timeout. These last two paragraphs sounded creepier than I thought. I need to clarify something: I wasn't there to loiter at the children's playground.

The playground just happened to be near the pickleball courts. That's what I was lusting after. Pickleball.

In Boca Raton, the South Florida city where I live, an outcry had occurred, much like it had in other cities far and wide. These outcries go something like this:

"We need pickleball courts," a small-but-vocal cabal of paddle-carrying super-voters say.

These tend to be the same people who complain that a 7-Eleven near their homes would attract "the wrong element." They're not shy.

"Pickleball? What's pickleball?"

"Don't worry," the zealots answer. "We will teach you how to play, because that's what we love to do. We could talk about pickleball all day."

And they do. Trust me. If you've got anywhere to be, don't invite a pickleball player to talk about the game.

Pickleball may seem like a simple game, but the minute pickleball players start explaining its mechanics, they have a knack of making it sound as complicated as astro physics.

And yet, they plow on, going heavy on the jargon to make it even more confusing. There's nothing pickleball disciples love more than explaining the "two bounce" rule to some hapless soul in the produce section of the supermarket.

"And would you like to know what the 'zero, zero, two' on my hat means?" a pickle person might ask.

Don't say, "yes." Run. If you're quick, you could get away before the inevitable subsequent primer on the pitfalls of "volleying from the kitchen."

I worry where this exuberant pickleball advocacy in our society is heading. I can see a day when pickleheads start going door to door on weekend mornings, knocking in search of new converts.

For when you play pickleball, you never can have too many potential doubles partners or opponents.

"Can I leave you with the new USAPB/IFP Official Rule Book pamphlet? It's got the updated service-let rule in it!"

Lock the doors. Hide behind the drapes. Don't move until you hear the squeaks of departing court shoes.

City officials in Boca Raton and elsewhere did what reasonable people would do when faced with a small, but determined group of citizens who care way too much about what on its surface seems way too little.

They caved to the zeal. And so the pickleball disciples in Boca Raton not only got four new courts in the new public park. They also got the city to reconfigure the tennis center by dismantling two tennis courts and converting that area to six pickleball courts. And then made plans to build another 12 courts there.

And that indoor basketball court in the community center? The one the kids' basketball league was using? Well, they double-purposed it by making it into pickleball courts too.

I found the pickleball courts in the park accidentally while taking a long walk with my wife during the first weeks of the COVID-19 pandemic.

After seeing those four fence-partitioned beauties, we ordered a cheap starter set of paddles and balls from Amazon, and started knocking the ball around. Just a little outdoor activity at a time when there was very little to do.

This wasn't my first brush with pickleball. I'm a newspaper columnist, which gives me a chance to occasionally experience other worlds just for the sake of describing them in columns.

Over the years, this has led to me trying out barroom sumo wrestling, belly dancing, and working as a sanitation worker on the back of a garbage truck.

For National Pickleball Month — yes, there is such a thing — in April of 2019, I played pickleball for the first time at a gated community where my friend Hap lived.

(By the way, Hap is an excellent pickleball name. Almost as good as Scooter or Rex, or for a woman, Ginger, Trixie or Mona.)

"When you grow up in Florida, you learn to swim," I wrote. "When you retire in Florida, you learn to play pickleball."

But this wasn't entirely true. The retirees at River Bridge told me that they were going into the public schools and teaching pickleball to the physical education teachers at 80 local middle schools and 50 elementary schools.

That was my first brush with pickleball evangelists. I had no idea there were so many of them, or that one day I too would become one.

I played that day with Hap and his buddies. But it seemed like just another one-off activity for a column. It was more fun than picking up garbage, but not as much fun as sumo wrestling. That was my judgment.

I broke a sweat, hit some balls, and never did figure out whose turn it was to serve or where to stand. In the end, I didn't see the magic. I drove away that day without an inkling that pickleball would be in my future.

But a year later, the coronavirus provided the pause, and pickleball stepped right in like an opportunistic virus attacking my compromised recreational immune system.

First, my wife and I just hit the ball back and forth. Then we played singles against each other, which isn't easy, especially with two beginning players.

This led to the inevitable. In pickleball, you can't help but arrive at playing the game the way it is best suited: As a doubles game.

That's where teamwork and court strategy come into play. The game becomes more textured and layered. It's not just getting the ball over the net. It's how and where you get it over the net, and what you're doing to anticipate the return.

And most important, with four players on a court that's only 44-feet long and 20-feet wide, just about every ball is no more than three steps away.

It's an action game, but the action is on a leash. Players unable to cover the expanse of a tennis court can usually get to where they need to go on a pickleball court.

People manage. And people wearing knee braces or others walking like they're auditioning for the lead in a community theater production of "Popeye" can still be fearsome pickleballers.

To borrow a line from the fictional Lt. Col. Bill Kilgore from the movie, *Apocalypse Now*, "I love the smell of Ben Gay in the morning."

Whether you're an athlete or not, it's a game that can be enjoyed at whatever skill level you're at. The ball, a plastic one with holes in it, doesn't travel as fast or as far as a tennis ball.

And yet, the way the game is designed to be played, points are often decided by quick exchanges of volleys between the two teams, with all four players facing each other inches beyond the non-volley-zone line, just 14 feet away from the player on the other side of the net.

It's a game of contradictions. It's slow and it's fast. It's simple and it's complex.

Some points end in an overhead smash, in what is clearly a power move. And yet the most prized shot in the game is a gentle, well-placed, low-arcing, slow-ball that ekes over the net, and is called a "dink."

And unlike most sports, the physiological differences between men and women don't matter. Pickleball doesn't favor size or strength. And players who are "bangers" — those who love to hit the ball as hard as possible — are routinely neutralized by skilled finesse players.

You can choose to just hit the ball around and enjoy the game on its most simple level. Or you can find yourself wanting to improve your game by exposing yourself to a nearly bottomless supply of instructional material.

If you're not careful, this can lead to hours of watching pickleball YouTube videos of tournament play, taking lessons from pickleball pros, and caring way too much about the lack of consistency in your "third-shot drop."

The game is also a social one.

To fully experience this game, you need to find other players. For couples, that means finding other couples who want to play.

Sometimes these couples are already playing. But a lot of times, you end up calling some friend you've been meaning to call for years.

"Hey, Lenny. This is Frank ... Frank Cerabino ... Good, and how are you and Sandy doing? ... Good ... Any knee injuries? ... No planters fasciitis? Great ... Still vertical? Terrific. Oh, I was just wondering ... "

Before long, you and your wife are both going through your contact lists to recruit all your able-bodied friends.

You also start writing down phone numbers of other couples you happen to see on the court who have similar abilities.

This is what happened to my wife and me. Jo and I developed a roster of other pickleball couples we could play, and we got memberships at the tennis center so we could reserve a pickleball court for 90 minutes at night.

We were playing nearly every weeknight from 7 to 8:30 p.m., against a different couple each night. And then on weekends, we'd show up at the park, where there were no reservations, but often lots of pickleball players looking for games during open play.

Some good pickle-couples for us materialized from these chance meetings on the public courts.

At the end of one of those chance meetings at the park, the woman in the other couple was entering our phone number in her phone, and I started to give my last name, and she waved me off.

"You're Frank Pickleball," she told me. "Almost everybody in my phone book now has the last name of 'Pickleball.'"

It didn't dawn on me that this was turning into what some people might consider an addiction until it became clear to me that playing pickleball every night wasn't enough pickleball for me.

It reminded me of an interview I did a long time ago with a great long-distance runner, who said that he ran so much that when he and his wife would take a car trip, it would bother him to see all that perfectly good roadway go by outside the car's window without running on it. So, his wife would occasionally let him out of the car and drive behind him on the shoulder of the road while he ran in front of the car for a few miles just to get it out of his system.

To play pickleball more than once a day, I would have to slip out of work early and find a couple of hours to play.

Many days, I'd play pickup games of pickleball in the park from 2 to 4:30 p.m, then race home, shower, eat dinner with my wife, and then we'd both go to the tennis center for 90 minutes of pickleball starting at 7 p.m.

I became embarrassed to tell the other couples during our nightly games that I had already logged in hours of pickleball earlier that day.

And I wasn't alone. There'd be others who always seemed to be playing, no matter where you were. And occasionally, I'd hear a snippet of conversation from another court from a player who announced that he might have gotten that ball, but he had already played earlier that day.

It wasn't as if I, alone, was experiencing this.

But it occurred to me that I was addicted on this one particular afternoon at the park. It was an especially hot, brutal South Florida afternoon. The temperature was near 90.

When I arrived at the court at 2 p.m., the worst time of day to play, only one of the four pickleball courts was being used. There were four women on it playing doubles.

I recognized them. They were regulars. And they were good. I played occasionally with a couple of them in pickup games, but they preferred to play with each other.

So, when I showed up, I sat down on the bench next to the courts and the playground. And I knew the pickleball foursome weren't going to make room for me to play with them.

The only way I'd get in that game was if one of the women got hurt, or had too much sun and needed a break.

But that hadn't happened that day. So they kept playing. One game would end, and another would start. And I just sat there, pretending not to care, and maybe fantasizing just a little about one of them pulling a muscle, or getting some non-surgical injury that caused her to call it a day.

I should have just gone home. After all, I was going to be playing again at 7 p.m. But I was ready. I had raced through my column that day just so I would have time for an afternoon session.

I had lathered myself up with sunscreen, brought my sweat towel, my bag with extra balls, if needed. And I had my new paddle out — the more expensive one I bought to replace that Amazon starter model.

With the players carrying on just fine without me, my only other hope was that other players, addicts just like me, would trickle in looking for action. And that was certainly possible.

It happens almost every day. You could count on a collection of random players showing up. Some would be pickleball teachers and terrific players. Others would be there for the first time. And then there'd be everything in between, a blend of all skill levels.

Sometimes the games were wildly lopsided. But most times, players sorted themselves out into games that were evenly matched and competitive. A lot of good games happened from this hodgepodge of arriving players.

But not on this day. For not only was it blisteringly hot. It was also very windy, the kind of day when balls hit from one side of the court tend to go long, and ones hit from the other side of the court barely make it over the net.

Between the wind and the heat, you'd have to be desperate to play. And I was.

So, I waited, fully expecting that my desperation would be shared by a new arrival, or that one of the women on the court would swoon, staggering for the shade, and ask if I'd jump in for a game.

But the afternoon just slipped away. And in time, the heat gave way to gray skies, and finally the first fat drops of an afternoon rainstorm that sent me scurrying to the parking lot.

I wasted an afternoon, hoping beyond hope to play this silly game for another time. Did I have a "pickleball problem"?

This would have been a golden opportunity for a group therapy session. I surely could have used one the moment I pulled out of the park, disappointed more than I would admit to myself, with my dry shirt and towel and my full water bottle.

"Hi, my name is Frank, and I am a pickleball addict," I would have said to a roomful of other sympathetic souls sitting in a circle in some conference room.

But I probably would have ruined the mood by adding, "By the way, are any of you free tomorrow afternoon at two?"

2

Finding Your Pickleball Partner

When you first venture bravely into the world of open-court pickleball, you may be alone.

If so, you're at the mercy of "the rack." Look for the rack. It's probably hanging on a fence near one of the courts.

Courts that don't have a rack probably have some other system, maybe a line of paddles with their handles stuck into the openings of a chain-link fence. Or a plastic bin where paddles are lined up on their edges in groups of four.

Either way, if you want to play on "open play" courts where time slots aren't reserved in advance, you'll need to use your paddle to announce your presence.

(If you have a popular paddle model, you may want to tape a tag to the side of your paddle with your name on it. It will eliminate any confusion about which paddle is yours when it comes time to decide who's up next.)

As new players arrive, they place their paddles in the slots of the rack. This is the way of taking your place at the end of the line.

Let's say the rack begins from the left side. The next time that players on a court finish their game, etiquette calls for them to relinquish the court to the next group of waiting players.

(The departing players may immediately put their paddles at the end of the rack and be playing again in a matter of minutes, considering that pickleball games typically last about 15 to 20 minutes.)

So, the owners of the first four paddles on the left become the players in the new doubles game starting on that newly vacant court.

If you come with a group, you may know the other three players. But if you arrive alone, and the courts are full of solo players that day, you'll be playing with a random grouping of other players. This can be fun, or it can be a complete bust if the skill levels are wildly different.

My wife, Jo, refers to this arrangement as "jungle ball."

This is why many players cultivate pickleball partners. It's a hedge against being marooned with disappointed players in a lopsided game.

Plus, showing up with a partner allows you both to warm up or play singles during those rare times when there's an empty court. Before long, some other suitable couple of opponents will show up, and you'll be in business.

Like squirrels looking for the perfect acorn, pickleballers are always foraging for court partners. The first likely subject in this search would be your significant other, your wife, the man or woman of your dreams.

This may be a mistake.

Sure, you may have promised to love and cherish that person for the rest of your life, 'til death do you part. But that doesn't mean he or she automatically gets grandfathered in as your pickleball partner.

That takes a little more discerning screening. Having sex is easy. Covering a lob isn't.

And just because your tax status is a joint filing, that's no reason to jump to conclusions here.

I have played with couples before who refuse to be the other's partner on the court. They'll play in the same game, but not as teammates.

In one instance, we had exhausted all the other combinations of the four players, and I finally said, "C'mon, just for one game, you two need to be partners."

And on the first volley, the husband drilled the wife in the back of the head while she was at the non-volley line and he was returning a groundstroke at the baseline.

"Oh," I said. "I see what you mean. Maybe this isn't a good idea."

As for me, I can report that things are working out fine so far with my wife on our pickleball partnership, but we have had years of off-the-court training.

And by that, I mean ballroom dance lessons.

To humor Jo one Christmas, I bought us eight dance lessons. One of my friends and his wife were going too.

It turned out that we were the only four people who showed up for what was supposed to be a large group class. The instructor, unwilling to put on his "Basie boots" for such a pitiful showing, sent us off to dinner, saying the dance classes were hereby canceled due to a lack of interest.

I wasn't sad. I was off the hook. At least, I thought I was.

But my wife later discovered another group dance class at a large performance space in another town, and there were more than enough people enrolled. I was boxed in. My friend and his wife bowed out. But there was no way for me to say "No." After all, this was my gift to Jo.

So, one night a week for eight weeks we learned the rudimentary steps of the rumba, tango and waltz.

When it was over, I thought I was done. But during the last class, the instructor said he could extend the lessons for another session at his more intimate private studio.

What started out as a class of 44 people, eventually got winnowed down to three couples, including us. And it went on in consecutive eight-week installments for three years.

I think the restaurant bar around the corner from the dance studio had something to do with it. And so our dancing lessons went on. And on. And on.

All from what was an 8-lesson dance class. The cautionary words in the *Gilligan's Island* TV show theme song — "A three hour tour!" — kept ringing in my head.

I'm not complaining. It turned out, we really liked ballroom dancing, even though at first it was more than frustrating. We had to learn to move seamlessly together, to be aware of slight movements, and to always stay connected.

And sometimes, to improvise and scramble a little to reset.

It turns out that pickleball, despite not having a cha-cha step, is a lot like ballroom dancing in that respect. The way to do it right is to flow with your partner and trust each other.

And you have to do a lot of moving in tandem, usually a side shuffle, (a little bit like a grapevine step) as your partner reaches and shifts for a cross-court dink.

Like ballroom dancing, if you and your partner don't stay synchronized and connected, bad things happen. In dancing, toes are stepped on. In pickleball, your opponents hit winners down the wide-open center of the court you've carelessly left unguarded.

You also learn to keep things in perspective. Despite our instructor's efforts to steer us toward dancing competitions, where people seek prizes for their ability to learn intricate dance routines, we were content to do it for fun.

Just let us practice our weekly lesson by twirling around the Polish-American Club on Sunday nights for a few foxtrots, between beer in plastic cups and a bottomless supply of popcorn, and we were happy.

That's the approach we share in pickleball — without the beer and popcorn.

We're not looking for titles or 5.0 ratings. We're happy with the thrills afforded by pickleball mediocrity. And don't underestimate the joys of pickleball mediocrity.

Pickleball mediocrity can be a lot of fun.

Do we want to get better? Sure. But we're not harboring any illusions here. We just love that we can find other couples who, like us, enjoy playing 90 minutes of pickleball on a regular basis.

One of the couples in our dance class that lasted the three years with us were two people who were not spouses or romantically involved with each other. They both had significant others who weren't interested in learning to dance.

This man and woman met each other in the dance class by chance and decided to be dance partners for years after that. It was a situation that worked for the both of them.

I mention this because maybe your perfect pickleball partner isn't your wife, husband, boyfriend or girlfriend.

Maybe there's a platonic paddler out there who is perfect for you. And all you need is the good fortune of crossing paths one day.

The important thing is that whomever your pickleball partner becomes, it's a good idea if you treat him or her with the kind of respect, attention and care that allows your relationship to stay strong.

In other words. Don't be a jerk to your pickleball partner.

I think I can get you started down this road. Here are six tips that will give you the best shot at making your pickleball relationship work.

Tip No. 1: The two of you are only into pickleball as much as the least-interested member of the couple. If you want to play five nights a week, and your partner is fine with one night a week, there may be a limit to your pickleball compatibility. Something's gotta give. Or you may require an open pickleball partnership.

And by that I mean, you may want to find another pickler on the side.

Tip No. 2: One of you is going to be better than the other one. If you're the more skilled partner, be careful how you behave.

This means there will be times during your game when your partner will make a mistake and lose a point by failing to return a ball that you are sure you would have hit back as a winner.

Never, never allow this to be expressed in either verbal or non-verbal communications. You may think you're a model of sportsmanship by not saying anything, but if you throw up your paddle, even for a second, or exhale audibly, you might as well have shouted, "I would have put that one away!"

Tip No. 3: No coaching on the court. If you pause the flow of a game to offer your partner a little tutorial on how he or she screwed up the last point, you are making things worse.

It's best to operate on the theory that everybody's doing as best as they can, and people know when they screw up.

On the other hand, "Would it kill you to step right up to the non-volley-zone line when the other team is serving to me!"

"Sorry. I didn't mean that. Sure, continue to stand back that extra foot and guarantee that more of your volleys will end up in the net as a result of your poor court placement."

"Oops, sorry again. I didn't mean that, either. I mean, yes I meant that, but I didn't mean to actually hear those words coming out of my mouth."

See what happens? It may look like a court, but it's a minefield.

Tip No. 4: If you ever "poach" a ball by reaching across the court to hit a ball that your partner could have clearly hit, and the ball you hit goes out, or is easily returned by the other team, apologize at the first break in play.

"I'm sorry," you should say. "I should have let you hit that. I got too carried away there. I'll try to be better next time."

Poaching is tricky. The best pickleball players poach a lot. And they don't get upset about it. It's routine, and part of the game for high-level players.

If you watch games among 5.0 players, which I'll admit, I do way too often, you'll frequently see the weakest player on each side being "targeted" by the other team.

"Targeting" means that the other team is trying to hit every ball to the weakest of the two opponents.

The more-skilled players get around this by pinching way over to the other side of his or her court, intentionally poaching anything hitable and daring the other team to try to hit one on the more open side of the court.

Like I said, this is part of the game at its highest levels. The weaker players expect it, and aren't upset by it.

But in recreational play, "targeting" can sometimes be seen as unsportsmanlike, or at least an area of friction in what otherwise would be a relaxing game.

You're all out there supposedly to have fun. There are no trophies or cash prizes for winning. And yet, in many rec games, you'll see a weak player being mercilessly targeted. Shot after shot is directed to him or her, while the more-skilled partner just stands there watching.

In games where the weaker player is obviously targeted, the stronger player is tempted to end his or her role as a spectator by reaching over to poach some of those balls heading for his or her partner.

Resist this temptation.

I say this from experience. I have been on both sides of this poaching experience in rec play. I've been the poacher and the poachee.

And I can report it's not good for your relationship with your partner to poach a ball and smash it brutishly into the back fence or a foot wide of the court. And it's even worse, to have your partner do that to you.

I try to make a conscious effort not to target the weaker player when I play. The key word in that sentence is "try."

My success in this endeavor usually is related to the score of the game and my view of humanity on the day in question.

If I'm feeling like Mother Teresa in an SPF-50 shirt and court shoes, I spread the love of my returns. But if I'm in my default mode, a cranky 66-year-old guy from South Florida waiting for the morning's psyllium husks to kick in, I've already sussed out who to target by the third serve.

Sorry, stranger. You caught me on a day when I wasn't the best person I could be. Incoming!

But I do think that, even if targeting is unsportsmanlike in rec play, it achieves something valuable: It makes the weaker player stronger by being given so many more opportunities to return balls than his or her partner.

I keep telling myself that. I'm not sure if I believe it yet, but it's helping.

The thing to remember here is that it's not the end of the world that your partner is being targeted. Try not to poach.

Unless you just can't help it. Sometimes, you gotta be bad. Who am I to judge?

Tip No. 5: The time to advise your partner not to hit a ball that's going out of bounds is while the ball is in flight before he or she has a chance to swing at it.

I write this as an offender of my own tip. I sometimes find myself after a rally is finished telling my partner, "You should have let that last one go. It was heading out."

That's jerk behavior. What I should have done was yell "No!" or "Let it go!" or "Bounce it!" while my partner was getting ready to hit the ball.

That's being a good partner. But if you miss your chance to advise your partner about a potential out-ball while the play is in progress, you ought to just clam up after the ball is dead.

If your partner asks you, "Was that one I hit going out?" after the rally, you can be honest.

But I don't recommend it.

"Maybe, but it's hard to say," is a better answer. "It was worth a try."

For the record, I plan to say that one day.

Tip No. 6: Have a heart-to-heart discussion about a difficult subject with your pickleball partner.

When considering a marriage partner, it helps to discuss your respective attitudes toward raising children before you say, "I do."

Similarly, in pickleball, there are things you should discuss with your partner before the two of you say, "Zero, zero, two."

I'm talking about the middle of the court. It's that place where neither of you are standing. It breaks up more pickleball relationships than anything else.

If you think games of pickleball are won and lost by the ability of players to zing accurate returns down the alleys, just nipping on or inside the sidelines, you haven't been watching or playing enough pickleball.

Points are routinely scored by well-placed balls between the two doubles partners down the middle of the court. It's almost meaningless for pickleball partners to say, "This is my side, and that's your side."

That's because there are too many balls that fall within an inch or two of that 15-foot-long center line that goes from the non-volley zone line to the baseline.

And some of those balls are angling diagonally across your side of the court, not traveling parallel to the sidelines.

If your focus is on trying to be the reincarnation of Emily Post on a pickleball court, you're going to screw up a lot of winnable points.

Instead of divining the precise landing spot of an incoming return in order to determine who is entitled to hit the ball back, you and your partner should know this in advance.

It will prevent what ranks as one of the most mortifying events in a pickleball game — and one that happens during many games.

It's that point in a rally when both teammates eye an incoming return down the middle of the court and assume it's the other person's ball. They'll both stand there, paddles frozen in the air, as the returnable ball bounces lazily between them without either player making a move to hit it.

The way to prevent this from happening is to have "the talk" with your pickleball partner before you start to play.

If you're both right-handed players, the player on the left side of the court as you're facing the net should, in most cases, take the middle balls because his or her forehand is naturally in the middle of the court.

Most players prefer their forehand, where they have more power and control than their backhand side.

The right-handed player on the right side of the court as you're facing the net would have to hit backhand shots for middle balls.

Things are a little more confusing when one player is left-handed, like me.

When I play with a right-handed partner, we both have forehand shots when the righty is on the left side of the court facing the net.

And neither of us have forehands when we switch sides.

This means we need to talk. This is my predicament when I play with my wife. Jo is right handed. It feels natural for both of us to want those middle balls when I'm on the right side of the court facing the net and she's on the left side.

And it also is tempting for the both of us to defer when we've switched sides.

How do we overcome this? I'd like to say that after 40-plus years of marriage we're like a fine-tuned watch that is so used to the two-as-one dynamic that we instinctively know when to follow through and when to back off.

But the truth is, we lose a lot of points this way. Even so, we haven't given up on each other.

Like dancing. It takes patience. And practice, and in the end, the fun you're having while doing it is all that matters.

And for that, it helps to find the right partner. Good luck.

3

The "Nice" People Game

There's a popular T-shirt you can buy on Amazon. It's available in nine colors, and it says, "The nicest people on Earth play pickleball."

That's not true, of course. I'm guessing the nicest people on Earth are those who give their service to others. And by service, I'm not talking about the kind that is delivered with an underhand motion below the navel with the wrist above the highest point of the paddle.

Conversely, if you're providing free dental and medical care to impoverished people in remote places with no access to health care services, you are in the running of being one of the "nicest people on Earth" even if you never set foot on a pickleball court.

Pickleball brands itself as a friendly sport. That's a good marketing move. But is that true? Not really.

People who play pickleball *are* often nice. But they could be nicer. I'll explain what I mean in a bit. But first, I'd like to note how the game, unlike most other sports, counts on players being fair and honest, which when you boil it down, is how nice people behave.

Pickleball players need to be nice, whether they like it or not, because it's baked into the game.

If you don't believe me, consider this: Imagine if baseball batters get to call their own balls and strikes.

The count is two balls and two strikes. The pitcher winds up and throws a curveball that breaks at the last moment, passing over the corner of home plate. The batter, frozen with indecision, watches the pitch as it thuds in the catcher's mitt behind him.

There's a momentary pause. The batter exhales and then says, "Good pitch. That was a strike. Strike three. I'm out."

That doesn't happen in baseball. But the equivalent of that happens every day in pickleball.

During a rally, an opponent hits a deep lob over your head, sending you scampering from the non-volley line to the baseline. The ball hits on or maybe just beyond the baseline while you make a futile attempt to hit it back, swatting it out of bounds or into the net.

The rules say that if you call it "out", you have to make the call promptly, which is defined as "prior to the ball being hit by the opponent, or before the ball becoming dead."

So, even though you took a swing at the ball, you still have an opportunity to quickly yell, "out." And if you don't, your partner in a doubles game also has the chance to yell, "out."

And if that's the case, that's the final call. The ball is officially "out."

It speaks of an ethos in pickleball that separates it from a lot of other sports.

In recreational games and tournament games without referees or line judges, which are the overwhelming majority of pickleball games, the line call is made by the team that is on the side of the court where the ball bounces.

That means that players are expected to make calls against their own interest, calls that happen frequently in the course of play. It's part of Pickleball's Code of Ethics.

"Players shall not call a ball 'out' unless they can clearly see a space between the line and the ball as it hits the ground," Rule 6.D.7 says.

This is my favorite rule in the game. It basically says that unless you clearly see that the ball hit to you is "out", you should play it as "in."

And what if the player striking the ball yells "out" as he or she hits it, but his or her doubles partner calls it "in"?

The rules spell that out too, saying that "then doubt exists and the team's call will be 'in.'"

If the receiving team isn't sure about the line call, and asks the players on the other side of the net what they thought about the ball's placement, it automatically forfeits the receiving team's ability to reject the other team's call if they say it was "in."

Also, a very Solomonic rule. The subtext of that rule says, we're allowing the receiving team an opportunity for honesty, but if they say they didn't see the call, then they have to abide by the other team's decision.

The upshot of these rules is that a lot of balls that are probably "out" should be considered "in", because there isn't a clear gap between the side of the pickleball and the baseline or sideline.

Considering that the balls are hard, and the point that they touch the court isn't on the outside edge of its side circumference, but somewhere closer to the line, it stands to reason that some "out" balls get to be "in."

I like to think of this as "The Princess Bride Rule."

If you've watched the movie, *The Princess Bride*, and you really should, Billy Crystal plays a character called Miracle Max, a Medieval medicine man who uses strange apothecary concoctions to bring people back from the dead.

"Your friend here is only mostly dead," Miracle Max says in the movie, after examining the lifeless body of the presumably dead hero.

"There's a big difference between mostly dead and all dead. Mostly dead is slightly alive," Max says. "With all dead, well there's usually only one thing you can do … Go through the clothes and look for loose change."

It would be fun to use Miracle Max's voice to explain a line call in pickleball.

"Your ball here is only 'mostly out,'" you could say. "There's a big difference between 'mostly out' and 'all out.' 'Mostly out' is 'slightly in.'"

A similar rule exists in the game of tennis, and the US Tennis Association code of ethics has a great way of summing this up.

"A ball 99 percent out is still 100 percent good," the USTA Code says.

The reason I like this pickleball rule so much is that it leads to longer rallies. To end a sustained and hard-fought rally on a marginal call is a crime against recreation. When we think back on a session of pickleball, the fondest memories are usually about those rallies that go on and on, often with dramatic moments and improbable "gets", and ending with an emphatic putaway or well-placed dink.

To short-circuit those moments by yelling "out" on a ball that was maybe "in", or at least really, really close to being "in", strikes me as a fun reducer.

And something "nice" people would naturally avoid.

The power of making calls against yourself in pickleball has odd manifestations. I've found that it's frequently a reap-what-you-sow situation.

If at the beginning of a game, one team starts calling a lot of close balls "out", there will be a time at the end of the game when that same team becomes tremendously disappointed to hear an "out" call for one of their returns that they saw as "in."

The converse is true. If you're more honest with your own calls, you just might get that favor repaid later in the game when the score is 8-8. Or maybe not.

I played with a woman once who had a very good way to calm herself down when she got a line call she didn't like from the other side of the court.

"It's only pickleball," she'd say aloud to herself. "It's only pickleball."

Now, *that* would make a good pickleball T-shirt.

***

While I'm on the subject of pickleball ethics, we might as well discuss the most contentious problem with the game, the part of pickleball that makes some players conclude that pickleball players aren't nice at all.

Due to the popularity of the sport, public courts are frequently crowded, and managing the traffic flow on the courts can be a point of contention between those playing and others waiting to play.

This, in some cases, has led to verbal altercations, and in rare instances, physical violence. For the most part, though, it has led to pickleball players feeling less than ... well ... nice.

Part of the problem is that the scarce resources of available courts are being shared by players who have vastly different levels of experience and athleticism. And when a court becomes open for the next four people waiting to play doubles, they're frequently not people who want to play with each other.

It reminds me of *Noon*, a one-act play by the great American playwright Terrence McNally. The play is a sexual farce about a bunch of people lured through a classified ad that invited them to show up at a particular apartment at noon for the promise of sexual adventure.

As the people show up, it becomes clear that they each have a particular sexual appetite that isn't shared by the others. Soon, the apartment is populated by people whose eagerness for sex is replaced by chaste frustration because the others there aren't interested in the particular kind of kinky sex they like.

Public pickleball courts can sometimes resemble that apartment in *Noon*. The courts can be full of people jonesing to play pickleball who grow frustrated because the other players there don't play pickleball the way they do. And that makes it harder for them to fulfill their pickleball fantasy.

I've come up with a technical term for this: *courtus interruptus.*

Here's a recent posting on the Pickleball Forum Facebook group that addresses this:

I currently play indoors and we have six courts set up five days a week. It's a great place to play and a really nice group of people. The issue is that we are getting a lot of beginners playing now and we are not sure what the best way to handle this is.

Most of us are willing to play at least one game with a beginner since we were all beginners at one time but sometimes we can get in a bad rotation that we can't get out of.

Presently, we have a plastic bin that we put our paddles in and then the next four players play and then the next four etc. At times we have chosen our own foursome to play with and we hold back our paddles until the players in front of us get to go, but that is making some people angry. I would love to hear how you all manage your courts.

To deal with this common complaint, some places have designated courts by ability.

So for example, Court No.1 will be available for the most skillful players, while Courts Nos. 2 and 3 will be available to players with intermediate skills, while Court No. 4 will be reserved for beginners.

But this doesn't work if people object, are blithely unaware of their own abilities, or just prefer to play with more skillful players.

After all, what we're talking about here is open play on public courts. Unlike courts that can be reserved due to memberships or residency requirements in a particular neighborhood, "open play" courts in public parks are, in a sense, "the people's courts" and everybody should have equal access to them.

But as the game gets more popular, the vast pool of intermediate players grows. So when beginners come along, they can feel like unwelcome arrivals. And being shunned leads them to conclude that despite what the T-shirts say, Pickleball isn't played by the "nicest people on Earth."

Or as one responder to that Pickleball Forum posting wrote:

"This is why I quit pickleball. How can a newbie ever get any better if no one ever wants to play with me?"

This problem is borne out in pickleball's otherwise cheery statistics.

USA Pickleball reported that 4.2 million people played pickleball in the year 2021, with 2.8 million of them "casual" players and 1.4 million of them "core" players.

A casual player is defined as somebody who played pickleball seven or fewer times in a year, while a core player got out on the courts at least eight times in a year.

The fact that casual players outnumbered core players ought to be seen as troubling. Instead of focusing on the overall 4.2 million people playing pickleball — a 21 percent growth over the previous year — the game's ambassadors ought to be drilling down on why two out of every three people who play pickleball try it for a little bit but don't get hooked to play more.

They all can't have developed planters fasciitis.

I think it has to do with court availability issues that sometimes bring a measure of resentment and stress to what ought to be an enjoyable couple of hours.

Here's how that stress sometimes happens.

I was listening to the Profound Pickleball podcast, which is the creation of Stephen Rahn, a former tennis player in Georgia who discovered pickleball in 2017, and became a self-described pickleball addict.

Rahn played pickleball "constantly", by his own reckoning, and has gradually become a 4.0-plus tournament player, a certified pickleball coach, and a pickleball podcaster.

On one episode of his podcast, Rahn went on an extended rant over differentiating between "open play" and "free play" on public courts.

Rahn said that "free play" means there's no expectation that you have to engage with others using the public courts. In other words, you and your group can play on the court without being pressured to break up your foursome and mix in with the others there.

"Now, if people are waiting, the county does expect us to give that court up after an hour if people are waiting," Rahn said on his podcast.

"So, let's say my foursome starts playing at 6 o'clock, and there's really not anybody else around, and we're playing. But then let's say at 6:30 a lot of people show up, and the other courts are then occupied," Rahn said.

"So, at the time the other courts are full, my private group has an hour to keep the courts if we so choose while people are waiting."

"Our time didn't start at 6. It started at 6:30 when the courts were full and there were people waiting," he said. "So we could if we wanted to play until 7:30 before we had to give up the court."

I disagree. I think that's being piggy with a public space. Do you see the problem with his interpretation of the one-hour rule?

Under Rahn's reasoning, all people showing up to play when the courts are full would be expected to wait for an hour before they would be able to step foot on any court.

I don't think that's fair, or very much in the spirit of a one-hour rule. I would think that the "nice" thing to do would be to give up the court to waiting players after you've played on it for one hour — no matter when those people started waiting.

And with that understanding in effect for the multiple courts there — each with its own starting time for players using it — players giving up the court would regain one of the courts again in a matter of minutes.

After playing pickleball for an hour, most players would welcome a water break and a short pause that in most cases lasts less than 15 minutes.

Holding a court for say 1 hour and 50 minutes because nobody was waiting for the first 50 minutes you started playing is abusing a public facility. At least it is to me, and I'm not all that nice.

Rahn complained in his podcast that he had been involved in this situation several times, where waiting people expected that his foursome of players would stop playing after holding the court for an hour.

I can't blame them. I would too.

"People sort of expect you to engage in 'open play' at all times, and they start asking you to rotate in and out," Rahn complained. "'Why aren't you stacking paddles? Why don't you let us play? Why don't you give us the court?'"

"They expect that 'open play' be all the time, and you should always be willing to rotate in and out, and I'm sorry, but that is not something that people always want to do."

Rahn bemoaned that this leads to waiting people "crowding the court and giving us the stink eye."

"We had to ask people to move back a few times," he said, recounting one incident. "People were walking behind the court while we were playing. I almost hit someone when I was about to serve because they were walking behind me."

"We ended up giving up the court before we had to in order to avoid any other potential negative situation," he said.

Rahn admitted that he used to like "open play" when he first started playing, but he doesn't like it anymore now that he likes to play with what he calls his "private group" on the public courts.

"That's how I learned to play pickleball," he said on the podcast. "It was mostly open play."

"But now, because at the level I play at, I've got a group of people, men and women, who are at a certain ability level. We like to play together and we don't often do 'open play' as much as maybe we used to."

As the interest in pickleball continues to outgrow its ability to generate available courts, this is an issue that won't go away, and one that will have a lot to do with determining how "nice" pickleball players really are.

***

There's another issue in pickleball that has popped up since the COVID-19 pandemic and it also, in a way, has to do with sportsmanship and the ethics of the sport.

Due to the virus, a provisional rule was added that allowed servers to place the ball on the paddle, sling it up in the air and hit it. A couple of professional players, Zane Navratil and Morgan Evans, experimented with this rule change and created what is now called "the chainsaw serve."

This serve, which imparts a double-spin on the ball, has spawned a lot of controversy in the pro ranks, mostly due to its ability to bedevil the best of players. The chainsaw serve has created multiple serving aces in a game that, unlike tennis, had been one marked by rules that limited the offensive capability of serves.

In the September 2021 Chicago Open, Zane Navratil used the chainsaw serve, getting four aces out of the first five serves in the Gold Medal mixed doubles match.

Michelle Esquivel, the pro who missed the first three service returns from Navratil, posted this on Facebook about the serve after the match.

"Some pros (notice very few) have found ways to take advantage of these new rule changes and used them to their advantage (Good for them, nothing wrong with that.)

"These rules were not made to evolve the serve, but to make it 'safer' and not touch the ball because of COVID.

"I could very well develop the same serve and work on getting ridiculous amounts of spin off the paddle and/or my paddle hand, but I chose not to.

"I do not believe in using the rule changes to make my serve 'tricky' for my opponents. When the ball hits the ground and spins to whatever direction the serve intended, it very much feels like 'jungle ball.'

"Sure, it's very innovative, works to the server's advantage in many ways . But I personally chose not to do it because I believe it ruins the game entirely. For all levels."

"I'm sure those who are currently using variations of the chainsaw serve are enjoying the advantages of these temporary rule changes, but I'm also hoping they won't last long. There are many ways to make your serve offensive with the original rules."

There has been significant lobbying, back and forth, about this rule.

Others have countered that the chainsaw serve should be allowed to remain as a natural development of skill in the relatively new sport. And that over time, people will learn to defend against it, and the game will grow because of it.

Morgan Evans wrote an open-letter defense of the serve, calling on pickleball's rules committee not to ban it.

"*The return of serve is a skill, and I believe we will stifle the development of that skill by taking away the most challenging serves. Creative serves force people to improve their return skills,*" Evans wrote.

"*Power is a skill. Spinning a ball is a skill. Accuracy is a skill. No one has ever been told that ball toss can't be a skill ...*

"*I'm not 220 pounds or an Israeli demi-god. But I'm good with my hands and that's what I use in order to compete in a rapidly deepening field.*

"*If you ban one serve that makes a serve better under the pretense that the game wasn't intended to have offensive serves, doesn't it then stand to reason that you must ban any type of offensive serve? Who wants to go down that road?*

"*There will be no serves with power, accuracy or spin. That doesn't sound like too much fun, does it? Imagine baseball without curve balls. Imagine tennis without the kick serve, basketball without the alley-oop.*"

As of this writing, there has been no official decision made on keeping or banning the "chainsaw" serve. Either way, it has created some consternation and controversy that's bound to linger.

***

Pickleball is very much in flux. Which is understandable. It has only been around since 1965, and didn't take off until decades later.

So, it's not unreasonable that, like other sports, it will modify itself as new generations of players test its limits and new opportunities for television audiences materialize and pressure the sport to be more spectator friendly.

Even the way pickleball games are scored may be subject to change. There's pressure on the sport to adopt "rally scoring", which would move games along more quickly.

Instead of points being scored by the serving side only, rally scoring awards points at the end of every rally, even when the receiving team wins the rally. Like in volleyball.

This would allow pickleball games to go to 21 or 25 points, and be played in more predictable times, which would accelerate the turnover of crowded courts and streamline tournament scheduling.

It would also end the double service, a common cause of confusion. Under rally scoring, each time a defending team wins a rally, it's a point for that team and a side out for the serving team. That means keeping score in doubles pickleball games will be remembering two numbers, not three.

But critics say, like the chainsaw serve, rally scoring would change the game in ways not intended.

For example, under the current rules, when a serving side player misses a third-shot drop, the penalty for doing that is a change in service, which at its worst case is a side out.

Under rally scoring, miss the relatively-risky third-shot drop and it's a point for the other side.

So, the ultimate effect of rally scoring may be a hesitancy of developing players to learn the tricky third-shot drop, which is a key part of the game as it stands now, and a gateway to the dinking facet of play.

Rally scoring may create a new emphasis on banging over dinking, which would make pickleball more like tennis and less like the defense-oriented game it has been.

And who wants that? Not me.

I like those drop shots, even when I hit them into the net and my partner says, "Nice try."

4

The New Shuffleboard

In one respect, pickleball is the new shuffleboard.

If you're a comedian, you trade in using well-understood generalities to make jokes.

For something to be funny, it has to be understated. So, for example, you don't call somebody "old", you just say "he eats the early-bird special" and that connects the dots for your audience.

Shuffleboard, like early-bird dinners, has long served as one of those comedic code words for old. Even in serious pieces.

An essay on aging in The New Yorker magazine published in 2017 talked about the perception of older people "creeping off into a twilit world of shuffleboard and sudoku."

These days, most shuffleboard courts are empty. Those stereotypical older people who used to play shuffleboard behind the guard gate entrances of their condo compounds are now playing pickleball.

And that has made pickleball the new shuffleboard, which means the comedic world is starting to use pickleball as its new stand-in for age-based humor.

Which turns out to be both right and wrong at the same time.

Pickleball and shuffleboard have similar origin stories. But they made radical departures in their development, very much like when early man ventured to walk on the ground while apes kept to the trees.

Pickleball is a recent newcomer to sports. And it started, more or less, by accident.

As the story goes, it was 1965, when a few dads from vacationing families in Bainbridge Island, Washington, crafted a driveway game to keep their bored kids busy during their gloomy-skied summer vacation.

Using a badminton net, a plastic ball, and paddles carved out of wood, businessman Bill Bell, Barney McCallum and their Congressman friend, Joel Pritchard, imagined the game and tinkered with it. They eventually brought their driveway court game back to Seattle, where it became part of Pitchard's campaign shtick.

As the story goes, the game was named after a family cocker spaniel, "Pickles", who liked to run after the errant balls. But like most charming stories, it turns out to be untrue.

At least according to Pickleball Magazine, which did a real investigative journalism piece on the name of the sport. Imagine that.

You've got your Woodward and Bernstein and the Watergate break-in on one end of the spectrum in your "journalism matters" folder and your Pickleball-coverup story on the other end.

The game's name, the magazine said, came from Pritchard's wife, Joan, and it was derived from the sport of crew. The rowers who weren't good enough to race in the more competitive boats were consigned to what was called "the pickle boat."

And so "pickleball" was a disparaging reference to the athletic abilities of the game's original players: the game played by the least athletic members of the team.

As for Pickles, the dog, well, Pickleball magazine did some Pulitzer-level research to debunk that theory. Starting with the undisputed fact that the game was called "pickleball" in 1965, the magazine went to work.

"Proof of when Pickles was born could help resolve the two-story name debate," wrote Wayne Dollard, the founder of Pickleball Magazine. "As the official magazine of pickleball, we decided to dig up the past and report the truth, regardless of the venerable feathers being ruffled."

Right on, Wayne!

"We looked for dog records, uncovered photos, and interviewed several people who were there from 1965-1970," he wrote. "Based on evidence, we learned that the dog was born in 1968 — three years after pickleball was first played and named."

I believe that's called uncovering the smoking spaniel.

Cute-dog story debunked. Once again proving the journalism axiom: Too much reporting gets in the way of a good story.

As for shuffleboard — the kind you play on the ground, not on a table in a bar — it has been around since at least the 13th Century, when it was played by King Henry the VIII of England.

(It must have taken a special kind of bravery to play against a guy who could simply arrange for your beheading after you beat him.)

Shuffleboard's origins are far less mysterious. And in other news, nobody really cares.

It landed here in America mostly in 55-and-over adult communities, where it provided vertical recreation and competitive opportunities for retirees who found it more doable than senior-league softball and more heart-healthy than canasta.

At first, pickleball seemed to be headed to a similar retirement community path. After those early pioneers of the game brought it to the Pacific Northwest, It took root mostly in the retirement communities of Arizona.

In 2001, pickleball made its debut at the Arizona Senior Olympics in an RV Park in Surprise, Arizona. It drew 100 players.

Since then it grew like crazy, mostly in the Southwest and Sunbelt states, with it becoming the most popular game in senior communities.

The National Senior Games Association, based in Surprise, Arizona, now has to cap pickleball participation in its annual games to 1,400 players.

But unlike shuffleboard, it didn't only appeal to aging Baby Boomers. Younger players have discovered pickleball, and it's changing the game.

Pickleball courts these days are being designed with larger footprints around them to allow harder-hitting, faster-running young players to return balls from out-of-bounds areas that older players could only dream of reaching.

As a result, the game has morphed to exist on multiple levels.

You might have a retirement-age foursome laughing and gently hitting rainbow shots over the net on one court. And then playing next to them are four 20-year-olds who are flying around the court, and posting near the non-volley line in an aggressive, percussive, display of quick reflexes that appears to be part of a different game.

Anna Leigh Waters began playing pickleball when she was 10 years old. Hurricane Irma had driven her and her mom to leave their Delray Beach, Florida, home and stay in Pennsylvania for two weeks.

That's when she played pickleball for the first time with her mom, Leigh Waters. From that experience, the mother and daughter teamed up to be a fearsome doubles team, and national champions within two years.

By the time she reached her teens, Anna Leigh Waters was already a decorated champion in singles, doubles and mixed doubles.

Professional pickleball player Ben Johns, who is ranked No. 1 in singles, doubles and mixed-doubles by the Pro Pickleball Association (PPA) turned 22 years old in 2021. He started placing in professional pickleball tournaments when he was 17.

These days, Franklin sells his signature paddle, while he and pickleball buddy Dekel Bar, age 27, have formed Pickleball Getaways, a company that puts together exotic pickleball-based vacations.

"By utilizing the unique backgrounds, skills, and knowledge of its team members, Pickleball Getaways provide exciting all-inclusive vacations combined with world-class pickleball instruction and organized recreational play," the company's website said. "We do all the travel planning so that our customers can show up with just their luggage and paddle for a unique and memorable trip."

The company's pickleball trips for the Summer of 2022 to Croatia and Portugal were sold out nearly a year in advance.

If you happen to be one of the world's best shuffleboard players, there aren't business and merchandising opportunities like this.

I know. I spoke to one of them.

Eric Hahmann, at 35 years old, is the youngest professional shuffleboard player in Florida. Hahmann who has been nationally ranked No. 2 in points and has won national tournaments isn't about to quit his day job.

"Can you make a living playing shuffleboard?" I asked.

"Oh, God no," he answered, then laughed.

Unlike pickleball, shuffleboard has remained mired in its retirement community past.

"The tournaments are still dominated by older people. There's more access to them for courts," Hahmann said. "Each retirement park has courts."

Hahmann is one of the leaders of the St. Petersburg Shuffleboard Club, which dates its founding to 1924 and bills itself as the oldest shuffleboard club in the world.

Today, it's the largest club too, with over 1,300 members, and Hahmann said they are having success in getting some young people to play.

But it's nothing like pickleball.

"It's the access," he said. "For shuffleboard, you need a decent grouping of courts. You need the sticks and discs and they have to be in good condition.

"Pickleball is at most parks. You can turn a tennis court into two pickleball courts," he said. "And people are more familiar with tennis than they are with shuffleboard."

There's also a merchandising issue. Pickleball is heavily merchandised with manufacturers relying on pro-player endorsements to sell products.

Take Tyson McGuffin, for example, one of the best pickleball players today.

McGuffin started out as a wrestler. He came from a family of wrestlers, and his father and brother were both wrestling coaches.

McGuffin graduated to tennis, and in his 20s made a living as a tennis coach while being ranked as one of the best tennis players in the state of Washington.

Then he found pickleball, which suited both his warrior gene cultivated through wrestling and his eye-hand-coordination that came from tennis. It took him all the way to national championships and the endorsement deals that followed.

McGuffin strikes quite a youthful pose: He's got an arm full of tattoos above his paddle hand, and a ball cap he likes to wear backwards.

He looks like a pickleball pirate, the kind of guy who would get a long, hard look from the security guard at your average retirement community.

But if you're trying to project youthful vigor to a middle-aged reservoir of pickleball-curious people, McGuffin's your guy.

He's one of the faces of Selkirk sports, a leading manufacturer of high-end pickleball paddles.

"Oh yeah, baby, this is it," McGuffin says in a promotional video while trying out one of the newer Selkirk models. "Oh. Love the precision. Love to be able to direct the ball anywhere I want on a dime.

"Love the added feel with some easy pop."

Like golfer Tiger Woods and tennis player Roger Federer, McGuffin has his own stylish monogram, which appears on his branded apparel sold by Selkirk.

I asked Hahmann if being what is essentially the Tyson McGuffin of shuffleboard has gotten him any similar promotional deals.

"There's no sponsor money in shuffleboard," Hahmann answered. "Nearly all of the equipment is made by one company in Florida, and they've been family owned for 90 years."

As pickleball grows in interest, aggressive merchandising has followed.

Tennis stores and apparel websites now feature pickleball items. You can buy court shoes that call themselves pickleball shoes, and tennis bracelets are now sold alongside pickleball bracelets, some with little dangling charms of hearts and paddles.

The Sports and Fitness Industry Association determined that in 2014 there were about 930,000 people who played pickleball eight or more times a year.

Over the next six years, that number of pickleball players who played more than eight times a year grew to 1.4 million players, while another 2.8 million casual players tried the sport — making it the fastest growing sport in America.

All the while, the average age of pickleball players has fallen to where it is now, about 38 years old.

The average age of players may be falling, but the majority of those dedicated players who play regularly are still 55 years old and above.

Take The Villages, for example. It's a sprawling adults-only retirement community in North Florida that spans three counties, covers 32 square miles, and is home to about 130,000 people.

Recreation in The Villages is paramount, and pickleball plays a starring role. There are reportedly 108 pickleball courts scattered throughout the communities there, and the calendar of tournaments at The Villages draw hundreds of players.

It's also home to a slew of pickleball clubs with colorful names such as Geezers and Gals, The Patient Picklers, and Bob's Bad Girls.

Shuffleboard is holding its own in The Villages, which touts its 187 courts, 800 players and 80 teams.

But outside these retirement communities, shuffleboard, unlike pickleball, seems to be withering.

The few times I've played shuffleboard at my community center courts, the rest of the courts in the eight-court complex were empty.

These two games may both serve as comedic premises for age-related humor. But they are on different trajectories.

USA Pickleball reports that the more than 8,700 pickleball courts are growing by 67 new courts every month. And that's not counting the home court I made in the street in front of my house.

Even the coronavirus pandemic, it seems, did nothing to stop the spread of the sport, with USA Pickleball claiming a 21 percent growth in new players during the first year of COVID-19.

I'm not surprised. After all, I was one of those new players.

"Have you tried playing pickleball?" I asked Hahmann, the shuffleboard pro.

"Yes, I have," he said. "A buddy of mine is really good at it."

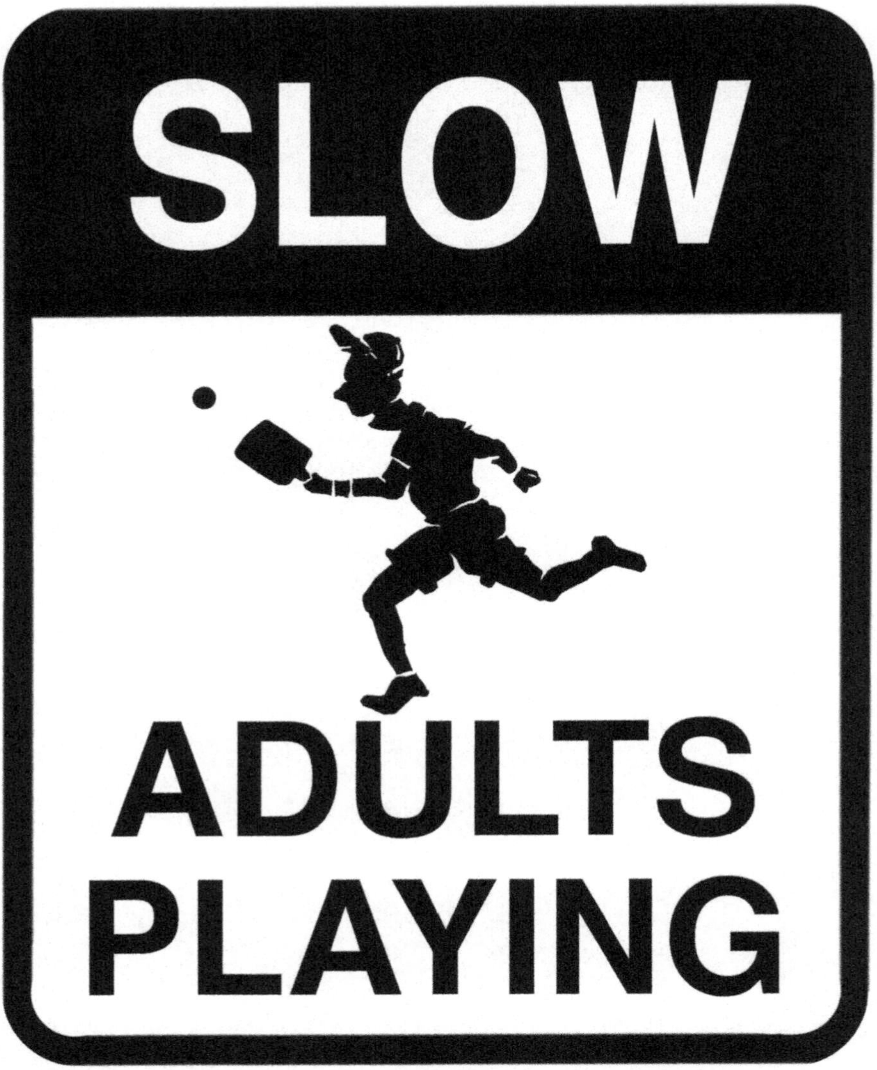
SLOW
ADULTS
PLAYING

5

Home Court Advantage

At first blush, it seemed like I had everything I needed when it came to pickleball "merch."

I climbed the economic ladder of paddles from an Amazon basic, to a mid-range Onix to a $200 Selkirk model. So, I'm good in the paddle department — at least until some over-hyped, heavily promoted $250 model hits the market with an endorsement by some pro who is half my age and says the new paddle has added two miles an hour to his volleys.

I'm a sucker for what has best been described as "the tyranny of small differences." I'm like one of those road cyclists who would spend hundreds of dollars extra on a tiny, lightweight titanium part for the bike, even though losing five pounds of belly fat would have far more dramatic results.

I can't log onto the Internet now without seeing some popup ad for pickleball-related merchandise I've perused and, like a lingering cough, can't shake.

I've bought court shoes in different colors to match the numerous shirts and shorts combinations I started ordering from Adidas, Fila, Nike, Prince and the rest.

But I'm still a little light on deep hues of green. And who knew how many shades of blue there were?

I've got an array of SPS-50 long-sleeved sun shirts in a rainbow of colors and a dozen various-hued ball caps to go along with them. And that doesn't count my two formal, not-for-play pickleball ball caps, the ones I wear when grocery shopping — my Boca Raton Pickleball Club cap and the novelty one that says "Just Dink It", with an embroidered yellow pickleball on the front.

Represent!

I also keep buying color-matching sport sunglasses in a way that suggests I may never conclude my search for the perfect pair. As a result I have a rabbit warren's worth of sunglasses, 20 pairs of them at last count. They've taken over the top of my dresser and have begun spilling out from under my tumbling mountain of ball caps.

Over the past year, I have also discovered the world of pickleball literature, which ranges from serious how-to books to ones that seem almost exclusively dedicated to making wisecracks about "the kitchen."

For my bathroom reading, pickleball has created a toilet-tank shift from poetry compilations and crossword puzzles to the latest issue of Pickleball Magazine and the eminently re-readable "The Art of Pickleball — Techniques and Strategies for Everyone" by Gale Leach.

The way I see it, I'm destined to either improve my game or develop hemorrhoids.

OK, what else? I have a tennis-ball hopper full of pickleballs for practice drills. Nothing fancy. Just something left over from one of my kids' old tennis days.

But that doesn't mean I haven't eyed the Lobster "Two Pickle" Ball Machine, a 42-pound rolling contraption that employs "2-line oscillation and electronic elevation."

I have no idea what that means, but it sounds like something I ought to have. And so does the idea of remotely firing 135 pickleballs from its wheelbarrow-sized well, with all sorts of spins and maximum ball speeds of 60 miles an hour.

But, I'm hitting the pause button on the Lobster for now.

For starters, when I think about all the balls it holds, I find myself focusing less on the part about hitting them with the paddle and more on the part about bending down afterwards to pick up 135 balls.

And then you've got to find someplace to park the pickleball cannon, which by the way, sells for an impressive $1,509 on the PickleballCentral.com website.

A guy can buy a lot more pairs of sunglasses and color-coordinated outfits with that kind of money.

OK, so I don't need the Lobster. At least that's what I've been telling myself.

But when my birthday rolled around this year, even though it seemed I had everything an obsessed pickleballer like me could want, I did find a big hole in my pickleball merch.

"I'm thinking of getting a portable net," I told my wife, and then added so she couldn't complain, "for my birthday."

Who's going to turn down a guy's only birthday wish? Especially once you hit 65, when with the proper acting skills, each birthday wish can take on the gravitas of a death row last-meal request.

So, yes, I got the net despite the fact that it is nearly impossible for me to play pickleball any more than I already do.

During weekday mornings, I usually play indoor pickleball at a community field house, which on those days converts its basketball gym to six pickleball courts. This is an open-play situation that draws dozens of regulars and the ability to play up to six hours of pickleball a day in an air-conditioned space away from the relentless South Florida sun.

I still do occasionally play outdoors during the week too — sun be damned. Especially when COVID cases start rising again.

Usually, three hours of indoor or outdoor pickleball during the day is enough. That's because I also play on weekday nights outdoors with my wife at the local tennis center, which allows members to reserve one of the six pickleball courts in 90-minute blocks.

We have a series of other couples we play doubles with each night from 7 to 8:30 p.m.

And then on weekends, we schedule more outdoor pickleball doubles, do drills at the tennis center, or nurse a little knee or shoulder soreness by taking a day or two off from pickleball.

(I know. Heresy!)

So, it might seem that the last thing I would need is a pickleball net of my own.

But that's what I got. I opted for SwiftNet 2.1 Portable Pickleball Net System. I fell for the 5-minute video done by pickleball pro Glen Peterson, who promoted the $369 portable net for its easy set up and ability to respond like a permanent net to those grazing shots near its perfectly situated 34-inch elevation at its center that follows a catenary curved path to the 36-inch height at either post.

Playing pickleball has, if nothing else, added the word "catenary" in my vocabulary.

I considered a more expensive net, one that had rolling feet. But it was three times the price, and besides, I don't have much time in the day to play yet another kind of pickleball.

However, there are times when it would be fun not to go anywhere to play. To just be able to walk outside the house and start playing with the neighbors on, say, a Saturday morning.

Just set up beach chairs on the front lawn for spectators, call a few ballers in the neighborhood and get up a game or two between the occasional car passing by.

The net's light enough for one person to pick it up and swing it to the side to let the car pass, as if it were a condominium's gated entrance.

(So far, no driver has intentionally tried to run over us or the net — a noteworthy detail if you know anything about Florida drivers.)

It struck me that I needed to get a portable net because the street in front of my home is pickleball perfect and lightly traveled (about one car every 15 minutes on weekends, according to unofficial empirical research.)

There's not much of a crown in the middle of the road, either, so it is nearly flat. And the pavement is still in good shape without any cracks that might create a weird bounce.

I give it a once-over with my cordless leaf blower, which knocks the little stones, dirt, leaves and other debris off the road … er, um … I mean, court, and I'm just about ready to go.

The big plus is that the street is about 21 feet wide, when measured from the edge of the grassy swale across the street to where the road ends and the swale begins in front of my house.

The width of a regulation pickleball court is 20 feet wide. So that means it fits perfectly on the street, with a buffer of a few inches along each sideline for the side posts of the portable net.

As for the other court dimensions, I needed to measure them out and mark them somehow. I considered chalk, but that seemed time consuming and far too temporary. I didn't like the idea of beginning each new session with a tape measure, and once again measuring and outlining the court.

Another option, drawing the outline of an entire court in spray paint would solve the temporary issue. But it might strike my city government (and maybe a cranky neighbor of two) as taking too much individual liberty with the public street.

I didn't want somebody dropping a dime on me to city code enforcement officers, who might cite me as a public menace, and get me saddled with some graffiti ordinance violation and an accumulation of daily fines.

I could see the headline: *"Boca Raton man sentenced to pickleball therapy in street defacement case."*

Or worse: *"Boca couple lose home over snowballing pickleball liens."*

I might have to agree to do some community service that involves warning school kids about the pitfalls of becoming a pickleball addict.

"I used to be an outstanding citizen. My home had once been singled out by the homeowner's association as 'Home of the Month.'"

"And then, almost overnight, I found myself a pariah on the block, just because I needed to clearly delineate the kitchen line. I mean, c'mon, you can't play pickleball without having a solid idea where the non-volley area begins and ends. Right, kids?"

So, I opted instead to permanently mark the street with small, easy-to-miss marks that delineated just the edges of key places in the court.

For the four corners, a black-spray painted "L" marked the edges. For the rest of the dimensions of the court, it was done cryptically with the net's placement (an N), and the 7-foot non-volley areas, and the two 10-foot halves marking the service boundaries, in spray-painted "T" markings — each only a couple inches big.

These spray-painted black marks are practically invisible to the untrained eye. But every time I look at the street now in front of my house, I see a pickleball court hiding in plain sight.

To quickly create the court, these spray-painted markers require some easy-to-put-down, easy-to-remove rubber strips to outline the court. To do that I bought the Franklin Sports Pickleball Court Marker Kit, four "L" shaped, 10-inch long pads to mark the corners, and eight "T" shaped pieces to mark the other parts of the court.

I found this was not enough to clearly mark the court. That there would need to be more visible markers between those 12 pieces. That could best be accomplished by some straight pieces of rubber to form the dashes that would outline the non-volley line and the boundaries for the service sides.

Franklin didn't make pickleball court dash-shaped markers. But Eco Walker did, so I bought two 10-packs of the 14.6-inch flat strips, which were more than enough to use.

Now, I had all I needed to turn a seemingly ordinary street into a well-marked, fairly realistic, regulation-size pickleball court in a matter of 10 minutes.

The makeshift court attracts neighbors, some of whom are curious enough to pick up a paddle and learn to play. And as a pickleball evangelist, I get great pleasure in having my own home court — as humble as it is, and as unimpressive as it may seem to the pickleball-indifferent among us.

This past summer, we even took the portable net on the road. My brothers, sister and I had planned a week-long family vacation at a beach house in North Carolina.

I couldn't imagine a week without pickleball.

So, as soon as we booked the house in North Topsail Beach, I began scouring online for nearby public pickleball courts.

It turned out that there were none in North Topsail Beach. But a 20-minute drive to the south, in Topsail Beach, there were two pickleball courts in a public park.

A news story about the pickleball courts said that the town was originally going to put a beach volleyball court in the park, but due to popular demand, two pickleball courts were built there instead. Another story about the growing popularity of pickleball.

We made the 20-minute drive to play on those courts, where we found other vacationing families doing the same thing.

It made more sense to stay at the beach house and play on our home court, which I mapped out at the house's big driveway.

Was it wide enough? No. There were planters filled with mulch that cut off part of the non-volley areas on both sides. Instead of a rectangular court, we ended up with a court that was skinny at the net and then arching out to its full width along the baselines. Like an hourglass.

It would have to do. And it did.

Each day, we'd move the net back in place, put down the rubber strips to mark the court and play again. It turns out our modified pickleball game, with rules made on the fly, can also be a lot of fun, enough fun to not consider driving the 20 minutes again to find the courts in the next town either in use, or temporarily out of commission due to a passing rain shower.

"Driveway pickle", as we called it, had no shortage of willing doubles teams ready to play. And as an added benefit, since playing there, I've developed a deeper appreciation for courts without mulch traps in their kitchens.

I started this topic by talking about pickleball merchandise, and as a result of getting the portable net, I've discovered the need for some other, yet to be sold, bit of pickleball gear that would be perfect for street pickleballers.

When we played recently, one of my pickleball neighbors found one of those big orange traffic cones in the neighborhood. He put it out in the middle of the street beyond the court to warn approaching cars of our game.

It looked pretty official. A couple of drivers seemed to think twice about driving on the block after seeing the orange cone. They backed up their cars and picked another street.

The cone got me thinking about other things that might be useful to deploy during street pickleball sessions.

Some of my neighbors have those plastic "slow children playing" signs to warn passing cars about kids playing on or near the street.

These signs, which usually include a green plastic man holding a red flag, not only warn motorists about children, but they also give grammarians a reason to discuss the importance of commas.

The "slow children playing" warning is not grammatically correct in the delivery of its message. Without a comma after the word "slow", the sign "slow children playing" implies that the children are slow, not that the motorists need to slow down.

Street pickleballers like me would probably buy their own motorist-warning signs for those times we are playing pickleball in the road.

"Slow adults playing pickleball" the signs could say.

And in the case of the pickleball sign, no comma would be necessary.

ASSAULT WITH
A DEADLY
BIRDBATH

VIOLATION
OF CITY NOISE
ORDINANCE

6

Taking a Dink out of Crime

When you think of pickleball, you probably don't think of crime. But maybe you should.

I was talking to Steve Downs, the deputy city manager of Orem, Utah.

Orem is a city of about 100,000 people that's 45 miles south of Salt Lake City. It calls itself "Family City, U.S.A" and takes pride in making the lists of the best places to live.

A few years ago, Downs and other city leaders decided to address a problem they saw in one of the city parks.

Sharon Park was the site of some furtive drug dealing, which was exacerbated by a portion of the park that was darkened by a canopy of trees.

Residents worried about the safety issue for kids who walk through the park to and from a nearby elementary school.

The city had about $300,000 to spend from a Community Development Block Grant, which could be used for neighborhood revitalization projects, economic development or an improvement in city services.

The revitalization of the park would be an acceptable use for those funds, city leaders reasoned.

"There were some barbecue grills, a playground and a pavilion," Downs said. "But it was underutilized. And with the trees, there was no light to it."

The solution: Get rid of some of the trees, put up lights for nighttime hours and run pickleball courts there from 6:30 a.m. to 10 p.m.

I guess you could call this, "Taking a dink out of crime."

It should not be a surprise that a town in Utah turned to pickleball. More than half the population of Orem are Mormons, members of the Church of Jesus Christ of Latter Day Saints.

The Mormons have become pickleball converts. The gym floors in their facilities are lined for pickleball. They've been spreading the word of pickleball wherever they go.

"The church is nudging its members toward physical fitness, and pickleball is on the church's list of approved sports because it is a game ideally suited to mixed doubles and intergenerational play," the Salt Lake City Weekly reported nine years ago.

Even little towns and cities in Utah have oversized pickleball footprints.

Spanish Fork, a town of about 40,000 people near Orem, built a complex with 16 outdoor public pickleball courts a few years ago.

St. George, a city of about 85,000 residents in Southwestern Utah, is home to the Little Valley Pickleball Complex, which features 24 lighted outdoor public courts that are open from 7 a.m. to 10 p.m. seven days a week, and have been used to host Western regional tournaments.

So when Orem built its first pickleball courts four years ago, it was following a trend — although the crime-fighting plan was new.

"We wanted to build eight courts, but some people wanted to keep more of the trees, so we ended up with six courts," Downs said.

The total cost, which included the lights and fencing, was about $600,000, which meant that the grant paid for half the project and the rest came out of the city fund.

It turned out to be a wise investment for the city, and a popular attraction that drew people there day and night.

Downs said it appeared that the pickleball courts had a profound influence on the crime issue there also. But he wanted to see if his impression was borne out by the crime stats.

"I had the police chief run the numbers for me after the park was open for a year," Downs said.

The numbers showed that drug calls in the park were down 40 percent. Half the fireworks complaints disappeared. Juvenile problems and police calls to the park were both down 60 percent. Thefts reported at the park dropped 57 percent.

"And it was used by people in all different demographics," Downs said.

"In the mornings, there'd be your real serious pickleball players," he said. "These were the players who would get in an hour before going to work."

"Then you get the ones during school time, which have been a blessing to the school. They are mostly the retirees, and it puts a lot of eyes on the park, which everybody likes," Downs said.

"If you go in the evenings, the pickleball courts are packed again, and this time it's the college students," Downs said.

The area is home to Brigham Young University and Utah Valley University.

"What I like about it is that it has drawn every generation there," Downs said.

Downs said pickleball made the park too popular for crime to happen there.

"There are just too many people there now for somebody to be doing something they shouldn't do," he said.

"Either we've got a bunch of reformed criminals who are now playing pickleball, or the criminals are doing something different."

A by-product of the courts was that it also brought others to the park, who used some of the area around the courts to play volleyball or spike ball, a game in which players take turns hitting a ball into a little trampoline.

Residents near the park who were crime weary appreciated the courts most of all.

"One of them told me that when he wakes up in the morning and hears the sound of pickleballs hitting the paddles, he feels safe.

"'Pickleball is the sound of safety and life,' he told me," Downs said.

The courts went over so well that Orem has added pickleball courts in two other parks.

As for Downs, 36, a former tennis player, the addition of the pickleball courts has turned him into a pickleballer.

"I liked it immediately," he said. "If I played tennis with people who knew how to play, I couldn't play with them. But with pickleball, unless you're playing somebody good, you can play with them."

While the residents near Orem's Sharon Park found the thwack, thwacking of pickleballs and paddles comforting, that experience hasn't been universal.

As pickleball's popularity has grown, it hasn't been universally embraced by those who find themselves living near the courts.

When they think of "crime", they think of themselves as the victims of crime to their ears by the nearby pickleball courts.

The sound of a plastic ball hitting a composite paddle is a short, but highly percussive sound.

Sound engineer Lance Willis, with the firm Speniaran and Willis, published an online paper that detailed the specific quality of the pickleball-paddle sound.

The peak sound, the study found, was short in duration, and quickly attenuating.

"The sound produced by the impact between a pickleball and paddle is characterized by a sudden onset and brief duration, typically on the order of two milliseconds for the direct path sound," the study said.

It compared the sound to "a sensation of pitch similar to a musical wood block percussion instrument."

When nearby homeowners complain about the sound, a few of these complaints have turned into lawsuits, and the lawsuits typically spur some sort of compromise involving sound buffering.

To hear some of the homeowners' complaints, you'd think that the Central Intelligence Agency could use pickleball court noise as an interrogation method for hard-to-crack terrorists.

Six years ago in Punta Gorda, Florida, the city converted tennis courts in its Gilchrist Park to eight pickleball courts. The people living across the street from that public park complained to city leaders. They said they couldn't stand being subjected to the sounds of pickleball all day and well into the night.

"It's that constant, banging, banging, banging all day long," resident Christie Federici , told a reporter from a local NBC-TV news station.

"A lot of stress, a lot of anxiety, a lot of frustration because it's constant," she said.

Her husband chimed in: "We sit there and say I hope it rains today just to quiet it down.

"My fun ends when their fun begins," he added.

Complaints like theirs frequently turn into demands for reduced hours of play, using softer balls, or constructing sound barriers to limit some of the noise.

And usually nobody is happy.

The homeowners in Punta Gorda played their own game of hardball with the city as their sound complaints lingered over a few years.

Two years ago, one of the nearby residents, Bernie DePaul, blamed the pickleball noise as the source of his stroke.

"The noise across the street was relatively constant," DePaul told the city council, according to a news report published by The Charlotte Sun. "I didn't need a medical doctor to tell me it was bothering me. It's been bothering me for years.

"When I went into the emergency room, the physician said there is nothing wrong with you ... we can't figure it out."

DePaul hired an acoustical engineer, William Thornton, of Thornton Acoustics and Vibrations, to write a report about pickleball noise in a paper presented to the city council.

Thornton wrote that pickleball noise "creates a human health risk" for people suffering from hypertension, heart disease and other ailments.

And he wrote that sound barriers won't help, the newspaper reported.

"There are no effective means (other than enclosing the entire pickleball court in a well-designed building) of reducing the noise emitted by the pickleball courts such as noise walls, barriers or screens," the report said. "Although these types of solutions are frequently suggested, they are not effective (for reasons of fundamental physics) and will not reduce the noise to acceptable levels."

Willis wasn't so absolute. Here's what he had to say about this:

"Based on our experience working with pickleball facilities, courts located within 350 feet of residential structures often require abatement. Courts located within 150 feet require careful abatement design to avoid complaints."

By "abatement" he means the construction of freestanding 8-foot walls near the pickleball courts to shield the paddle noise from nearby residents.

"The cost of the walls can be reduced by lowering the courts into the ground and using the excess soil to build a berm around the courts," he wrote. "Placing the wall on top of the berm will lower the required height of the wall itself, reducing construction costs."

The wall could be masonry of solid fence system with enough mass to insulate the sound, he wrote.

"For pickleball courts located in the middle of a residential area with houses on more than two sides, screen walls may be required on opposite sides of the courts. When these walls are parallel to each other, reflections between them can degrade the performance of the walls significantly.

"In this case, sound absorbing panels may need to be installed on one or both walls to stop multiple reflections from amplifying the sound going over the walls. This can almost double the cost of the walls and may make the site financially unfeasible," he wrote.

And how the courts are oriented also matters. The sound tends to spread more in the direction of play, rather than to the sides of the pickleball courts.

"By positioning the courts so that the line of the net runs through the most noise sensitive area, a noticeable reduction in sound pressure level can be achieved at this location," he wrote.

In Ridgewood, New Jersey, pickleball in the public parks there has turned neighbor against neighbor due to noise complaints. The Village Council responded by spending $20,000 in noise blocking fencing, mandating that quieter "green zone" designated paddles be used, and limiting the times that pickleball could be played.

These time restrictions included banning pickleball for two days each week, and for the rest of the days banning play before 10 a.m. and ending play no later than 5 p.m.

The village also began charging pickleballers $20 annual memberships to use the courts, which had been free, and using a parks employee to function as a security guard to make sure that no players were violating the restrictions.

Who knew pickleball was this complicated?

And what about playing with spongy, soft balls that don't make that sharp thwacking sound? They don't play the same way as traditional pickleballs do, which are seamless plastic balls made through a molded one-piece process.

Outdoor balls have more holes than indoor balls, and the holes are smaller, so the ball is less susceptible to the wind. They are also heavier, harder and thicker, which helps accentuate the loud thwack when they are struck hard.

Non-players say the easy solution to the noise would be to adopt a softer ball replacement that doesn't make much sound. But those balls, which are available, play differently than traditional balls and are not sanctioned for tournaments.

If you go to PickleballCentral.com, a pickle-centric marketplace for pickleball items, it lists the GAMMA Foam Quiet Ball among its offerings.

The customer comments tell a story. When you read them you'll find a bunch of players who were told by their communities that they couldn't play pickleball unless they used the quieter balls.

You'll also see comments about how the foam balls perform differently than the traditional pickleballs.

"I've been using these in my garage so that I don't drive my wife crazy while doing wall ball practice," one buyer wrote. "These work pretty well. They feel heavier and bounce higher than the typical ball, but they are close enough for my practice needs."

My favorite comment was this one:

"We have a group of 10 avid players and we just couldn't deal with no-impact noise! The flight of the ball was fine but no sound didn't get it for us!"

So, while some people living in the vicinity of courts were complaining that the sound of pickleballs striking paddles from hundreds of feet away was too much to bear, pickleball players standing in the midst of all that thwacking found that losing the familiar rat-a-tat sounds of play to be an aspect of the game they wanted back.

For the people living near courts it's the sound of safety and life for some, and the sound of hypertension and death of others.

And for those holding the paddles on the court, it's the sound of the game itself.

Go figure.

One thing seems clear: As new communities are built and tennis courts continue to yield to pickleball courts, it makes sense to design them with the kind of sound engineering principles that will eliminate the need for both lawsuits and foam balls.

7

Pilgrims with Paddles

While hanging around the fringes of the pickleball courts, chances are you're going to hear somebody start talking about "Naples."

OK, probably not at first. Maybe after some monologuing about a muscle cream, or complaints about (a) the wind (b) the sun (c) the humidity, or (d) "the young people" on Court Number 3.

But eventually, somebody's going to say it:

"Have you been to Naples?"

I imagine that this is similar to what concert violinists say, except that they ask about Carnegie Hall, not a small city in Southwest Florida.

Naples, Florida, is an out-of-the-way place with a hucksterish past. But there's no single place on Earth that has more pickleball courts than the 64 in a single Naples' facility, grandly named the Pickleball Academy of Southwest Florida.

That this hub of pickleball ended up in Naples is something both surprising on one level, and understandable on another.

The city was founded in the late 19th century by a couple of enterprising businessmen from Kentucky: One of them was John Williams, a former Confederate Army general known as "Cerro Gordo", a name derived from his exploits in a previous Mexican-American war battle of that name. After the Civil War Williams served a term as a U.S. Senator from Kentucky before turning a business eye to Florida. His partner was Walter Halderman, the publisher of The Louisville Courier-Journal newspaper.

Both men joined the land development rush to Florida in the 1880s, a time when the relatively new state was a vast, green swamp for the taking.

What today is the third most populous state was a patchwork of small towns, mostly along the coasts. Even by 1900, Jacksonville, Pensacola, Key West, and Tampa were the only cities in Florida that had more than 10,000 residents. Orlando had lots of oranges, but fewer than 2,500 people. And Miami had just 400 residents until Henry Flagler's railroad reached there in 1896.

Florida became the 27th state in 1845, but 40 years later it was still mostly seen by outsiders as inhospitable for human habitation. The entire population of the state amounted to fewer than 300,000 people.

But developers up North saw an opportunity. Something called the Swamp and Overflowed Lands Act of 1850 put 20 million acres of Florida land under state control.

To keep the state from going bankrupt, Florida officials sold that land, some of it under water, to real estate speculators on the cheap. And they started buying enormous hunks of Florida with the idea of selling the swamp land to individual buyers.

All it took was some hyped-up salesmanship to convince the buyers that the land they were getting, sight unseen, was a sliver of warm-weather paradise.

One Philadelphia businessman, Hamilton Disson, bought 4 million acres of Florida for 25 cents an acre. His plan was to drain the Everglades to make the Southern end of Florida fit for more than alligators.

Williams and Halderman imagined the Gulfside area in Southwest Florida as a prime location for sportsmen looking for an unspoiled getaway to hunt and fish. Halderman's newspaper called it a spot in Florida that surpassed Naples, Italy, in the beauty of its waterfront. The two developers created the Naples Company and the town became known as Naples.

There were about 80 people living there when a pier and the first hotel was built in 1889.

The only way to get to this remote Florida outpost was by boat, which only helped its appeal to rich Northerners looking for an exclusive, exotic adventure here in the states.

"Naples is not a resort, but to the fisher and the hunter, Naples is virgin; the forests and the jungles are scarce trodden, the waters, as it were, untouched," a piece in Halderman's Courier-Journal proclaimed. "Fancy people condemned to live on venison and bronzed wild turkey, pompano and sure enough oysters — and such turkeys! And such oysters!"

Eventually, Naples got swallowed up by Collier County, named for the Memphis advertiser, Barron Collier, who made his fortune selling streetcar ads.

Collier became the biggest landowner in Florida in the early 20th Century after visiting Southwest Florida for the first time in 1911. He bought up one million acres of land and brought telephone and railroad service to the area.

While Florida's population exploded during the 20th century, especially in cities on Florida's 1,350 miles of coastline, Naples remained a relatively small town on the state's Gulf coast.

Today, there are 181 cities in Florida that have a bigger population than Naples' approximately 22,000 residents.

At first glance, it might seem that nothing important happens in Naples. Tourism is still the biggest industry. The median age is 61 — 19 years older than the state's median age. And Naples' downtown area is full of wealth management offices, a testament to the numbers of people who are living off their investments.

It's mostly a posh, manicured corner of Florida beckoning to financially comfortable, newly-retired people to come for at least part of the year.

Florida's retiree population sorts by the divergent paths of the state's two main interstate highways. Interstate 75 drains the Midwest into Florida's Gulf Coast, while Interstate 95 pulls Northeasterners down to the ocean side of Florida's coastline.

The people who once drove south on those roads for family vacations would later in life come back to their Florida vacation haunts to retire.

As a result, Naples is full of mild-mannered, well-off Midwesterners who are "people of color" only if you consider varying shades of beige to be your palette.

And they take their "Naples" name way too seriously. The little downtown area along 5th Avenue South is full of Italian restaurants. It's hard to find a restaurant that isn't an Italian restaurant in Naples.

And while visiting on a busy Friday night, I couldn't help noticing the three busking musicians who were playing for tips on the downtown sidewalks.

All of them were playing accordions. A town of accordion buskers. Imagine that.

One of them was playing the Beatles song, "When I'm 64," an optimistic selection coming from a squeezebox player who was well beyond that age.

That's Naples.

"It's like Disneyworld without the rides," was how my wife summed up Naples.

We made the pilgrimage to Naples not to eat lasagna, but to play pickleball. When I wrote that "nothing important seems to happen" in Naples, I was leaving some wiggle room for pickleball.

Because if you think pickleball is important — and you definitely should — then Naples is a much larger dot on the map than it may appear to be.

After all, Naples is home to the Pickleball Academy of Southwest Florida. If you follow tournament pickleball — and you definitely should not — you'll see that this facility has been home to the U.S. Open Pickleball Championships since 2016.

And it's slated to continue holding the U.S. Open there through 2025. If you watch YouTube videos of highlights from professional pickleball matches, you're going to be watching games that have been played in Naples.

And it's not just pro pickleball that happens in Naples.

The Academy calls itself "the premiere training academy for pickleball lessons and activities of all ages and skill levels. From beginner to advanced clinics, to private and semi-private lessons; including destination camps, team building programs and tournaments throughout the year."

And as I previously mentioned, it has 64 courts. How can you not want to play pickleball at a place that has that many courts?

So, Jo and I made it a pickleball destination weekend. I was checking "Mecca" off my pickleball bucket list.

First step, call Jerry Pershing. I found his number on the academy website and gave him a call.

"Is this Frank Cerabino?" he asked, reading my name off the caller ID, as if he knew me. "I've been expecting your call."

"Yes," I answered. "Is this Jerry Pershing?"

We were off to a rollicking start. We didn't know each other, but Jerry and I kept going back and forth, looking for conversational lobs to return with verbal slams.

I explained that I was calling to book my wife and myself for a lesson with him.

"How did you get my name?" he asked.

"There were five pros listed and you had the best pickleball name," I said. "Jerry Pershing. Are you related to the general?"

"You know, there are lots of people who aren't old enough to get that reference," he says.

Gen. John "Black Jack" Pershing led the American Expeditionary Front on the Western Front during World War I.

"Pickleball is the one sport where World War I history might register," I said.

Pershing, the one who was the general, said: "If you know how to shoot, and are quite ready to shoot, the chances are that you won't have to shoot."

Pershing, the pickleball pro said: "Bring sunscreen and water. It gets hot out here."

I guess you could say that these unrelated Pershing men shared a zeal for proper preparation for battle.

As for the facility, the word "academy" conjures up a Hogwarts-like setting, something with an impressive entrance at least.

But the Pickleball Academy of Southwest Florida is true to the state's history of hyperbolic salesmanship.

It's actually just something you find in the back of the East Naples Community Park, an otherwise unremarkable county park in the unglamourous part of town.

East Naples is basically West Everglades, a testament to Florida's knack for creating sprawl with new developments pushing deeper into the state's watery interior.

The East Naples Community Park looks unremarkable from the street. When you turn in, it's just ball fields, racketball and shuffleboard courts.

All empty on the Saturday morning Jo and I arrived.

There's no grand pickleball sign out front by the street, either. You just pull into the park, wind down the main road and keep going until it ends, and the large expanse of pickleball courts reveal themselves.

That's when you see a large shade structure that covers its center-court matches and provides seating for up to 1,200 people.

And off to the right there are a couple of small blockhouse-style buildings that house the restrooms and the pro shop.

But mostly, it's just lots of pickleball courts divided by a maze of chain-link fencing.

If you went there a decade ago, you'd have seen a skateboarding facility and a roller rink there.

"About 10 or 11 years ago, there were four temporary courts in all of Naples," Jim Ludwig told me.

Ludwig, one of founding architects of Naples' pickleball empire, now runs a charity called "Pickleball for All," a group that is responsible for putting pickleball paddles in the hands of every kid in the Collier County Public Schools system.

The group raises money to provide schools with pickleball kits, which include 40 paddles, six dozen pickleballs, two nets, temporary line markers, chalk, tape and instructions.

In 2015, Ludwig partnered with Terri Graham and Chris Evon to pitch local tourism officials on a vision of Naples as the East Coast hub of pickleball, a sport that had been far more popular in the American Southwest.

National tournaments were in Arizona, not Florida.

Ludwig's team told local tourism officials they could have national pickleball championships right there in Naples, the first championship matches on the East Coast, if they had a suitable facility. And the idea hit home.

The county put up $150,000 in tourism tax dollars to get things started.

"The county is so excited about being the host for the first pickleball championships," Collier County commissioner Donna Fiala told The Naples Daily News in September of 2015. "We're going to see one of the main focuses of this park be pickleball."

The construction of permanent courts at the county park took off in anticipation of the first U.S. Open being held there the following year.

The academy grew not only from the success of holding the U.S. Open Pickleball Championships in the park in 2016, but also the ability of organizers to recruit one of the top players in the game to relocate to Naples and become the head instructor.

Simone Jardim resigned as Michigan State University's women's tennis coach to become the top pickleball pro at the Naples facility, which started holding instructional camps.

Jardim, who is from Brazil, moved to Naples because of the climate. And as a player-pro she has remained at or near the top of the national pickleball rankings in both singles and doubles.

Getting somebody of her calibre to teach classes there and sing the praises of Naples helped legitimize the area and the facility.

There are four major pickleball tournaments held at the facility each year, including the U.S. Open, which is under contract to be there through 2025.

What started as a little pickleball operation is now the largest pickleball facility in the world, where pros and recreation players come to play.

"During the season we get 400 to 500 players playing during the day and 200 to 300 at night," Ludwig said.

Pickleball's reigning champion, Ben Johns, 22, started playing there as a teenage tennis player, and was quickly recruited by Ludwig's wife.

"My wife said, 'You got to come here and see this kid'" Ludwig said. "Well, to my wife, everybody's a 5.0 player because she's a beginner."

Ludwig watched Johns playing with his father, and he quickly saw that his wife was right. Johns was special.

"He was a banger. He was playing like a tennis player," Ludwig said. "So, I jumped in and showed him the dink game."

And then he put Johns under the tutelage of pro Kyle Yates, who was also instrumental in promoting Naples.

"Four years later, Ben is making $250,000 a year playing pickleball," Ludwig said.

And Yates would become Johns' doubles partner, teaming up with him to win pro men's doubles tournaments.

As Naples started becoming synonymous with pickleball, the facility kept growing. A giant welcome center is under construction now.

It's going to include restrooms, showers for players, and an expanded pro shop. There's going to be a food truck area where players can get something to eat without having to leave the park.

And the racquetball courts in the park will be removed to accommodate a covered pickleball stadium that will seat up to 4,000 people, Ludwig said.

The academy's success has caused the county to move the other activities out of the park to let pickleball take over more land there.

"We're going to have to find another place for the soccer fields, because we're going to need more land for pickleball parking," Jack Wert, Collier County's tourism director, told me.

"We're at capacity now, and if we keep growing, we're going to have to find a way to relocate all the other sports for pickleball."

The park has created a community of pickleballers.

"The other thing we're seeing with pickleball in Naples is that whenever new homes are being built, in virtually every development, they are including at least two or four pickleball courts," Wert said.

"It's growing dramatically."

There's also a bit of a pickleball arms race going on in Southwest Florida. Jardim and her husband Chad Edwards have moved on from the Naples facility to the Peak Performance Pickleball Academy, just a half-hour drive away up the coast in Bonita Springs.

Peak Performance holds tournaments, clinics and lessons. The Naples center can't rest on its laurels.

While Jo and I took our early-Saturday-morning, 90-minute lesson at the Naples facility with "Coach Jerry", players started showing up and filling the courts.

The familiar "thwack, thwack" sounds of pickleball paddles filled the air as we progressed through the lesson.

Afterwards, we were warmed up and ready to play some games. The courts there are segregated by ability. Coach Jerry sent us to the 3.0 courts to play.

In that section of courts, there were two chain-link-divided rows of five courts, with a central corridor between each row.

Waiting players milled around the near end of the courts, looking at a dry-erase board that was checkerboarded into rectangles.

If you wanted to play, you used a black marker to write your first name in the first available rectangle that didn't already have four names written in it.

As a game ended on the courts, the next rectangle of players were up, and as they left to play, somebody would draw an X over the block to denote that they were no longer waiting.

Even though the courts were packed, with 10 courts in play, we didn't have to wait long. As for the rankings, well, players just decide how good they are.

After playing a few games against players with a wide range of abilities, I got the sense that some of the players were either 3.5 players who liked to win all the time, or 2.5 players who didn't want to play on the 2.5 courts.

If you play on the courts there reserved for 4.0 players or higher, you can only get on if your skill level has been certified.

"I started that because I was a better player getting stuck playing with not-so-good players," Ludwig said. "And that just intimidates everybody."

Ludwig said the next step will be to require certification on the 3.5 courts, and then work down to the 3.0 courts.

But for now, the 3.0 courts are on the honor system. The good part about pickleball is that even if it's a lopsided game, it lasts about as long as a Florida afternoon thunderstorm.

Fifteen minutes later and you're done. It was terrific to be able to play so many games against so many people in such an efficient manner.

And being that this was Naples, they were mostly friendly people in their 60s oozing with Midwestern jocularity on their faces, Italian restaurant food in their bellies, and well-concealed competitiveness in their souls.

"Call me Stingray," one guy named Ray told me. "That's my pickleball name. What's your pickleball name?"

"I don't have a pickleball name," I said. "Are you supposed to have a pickleball name?"

By about noon, the heat of the day thinned out the crowds until Jo and I were a couple of the last remaining people on the courts.

Done for the day, but back again on Sunday for another morning of endless pickleball with the Naplesvillians.

Oh, I said to Jo, how sweet would it be for our pickleball game to live in Naples. (And I already know how to play the accordion!)

Then again, I don't know what would get me first: the knees or the pasta.

Mecca. Check.

8

Pickleball A to Z

A is for "aggro dinking"

Definition: This is pickleball slang for aggressive dinking on the non-volley line. It's the kind of dink-battle shot that makes your opponent have to shuffle to the side or reach with a backhand to return the dink to you.

The object of aggro dinking is to force a pop-up return that allows you to break the back-and-forth gentle returns over the net with a hard volley for a winner. Maybe even a meat volley.

Used in a sentence: "He third-shot dropped me, which led to a dink battle that ended when I aggro dinked him into a pop up."

***

B is for "banger"

Definition: A banger is a player who thrives on hitting high-velocity groundstrokes and volleys while avoiding dinks.

Bangers try to overpower and intimidate their opponents with hard-hit balls, often considering third-shot drops and other dinking behavior to be unmanly, boring or a sign of weakness.

Used in a sentence: "I refused to get in a firefight with that banger."

***

C is for "carry"

Definition: A "carry" is a shot that slides along the face of a pickleball paddle rather than making a clean single strike.

Used in a sentence: "It's legal to carry a shot in pickleball."

***

D is for "dead dink"

Definition: An ineffective dink that doesn't make your opponent move or reach to his or her side. It's a squandered opportunity to hit an unattackable dink that can sometimes result in a ball hit into the net, or a pop-up that will allow you to slam the return.

Used in a sentence: "I was ready for his third-shot drop, but unfortunately, I responded with a dead dink instead of one that would have sent him reaching with his backhand."

***

E is for "Erne"

Definition: This is a difficult pickleball shot named after Erne Perry, the player who popularized it.

An Erne is accomplished by jumping or stepping outside the non-volley zone, ending up on the side of the court to volley a ball to the other side, often around the outside of the post.

For it to be legal, your feet must be outside the kitchen area, and you have to hit the ball when it is on your side of the net without making any contact with the net.

Used in a sentence: "In order to be good at an Erne, you have to jump outside the non-volley zone before the player on the other team hits the ball."

***

F is for "falafel"

Definition: a shot that comes dead off the paddle and falls short of the net.

Used in a sentence: "It was a terrific rally that deserved a better ending than that falafel I hit."

***

G is for "getting pickled"

Definition: Getting pickled is losing a game 11-0.

Used in a sentence: "I started taking lessons because I was tired of getting pickled at the community center courts."

***

H is for "half-volley"

Definition: A half-volley is when you hit the ball just after it bounces on the court, striking it as it ascends on its arc.

Used in a sentence: "When I got caught in no-man's-land, I was forced to half-volley a return before I could make it to the non-volley line."

***

I is for "indoor pickleball"

Definition: This is a pickleball with 26 holes, instead of the 40 holes on an outdoor pickleball. Indoor pickleballs are softer than outdoor balls and tend to bounce higher.

Used in a sentence: "I find it harder to hit unattackable dinks with an indoor pickleball."

***

J is for "Jugs."

Definition: No, not that! Get your mind out of the gutter. Jugs is a top-selling indoor pickleball brand.

Used in a sentence: "I've ordered new Jugs from Amazon."

***

K is for "kitchen"

Definition: The slang term for the seven-foot-wide non-volley zone measured from the net.

Despite the implication that you've got to "stay out of the kitchen", there's no prohibition to standing in the kitchen at any time during the game. You just can't volley a ball while you're standing in it or on the line.

Used in a sentence: "It's a fault if the momentum from your slam carries you into the kitchen."

***

L is for "little-bit long"

Definition: Any shot by an opponent that may be on the line, but you're not willing to concede the point without further discussion.

Used in a sentence: "Looked a little-bit long to me, Janice. What do you think?"

***

M is for "meat volley"

Definition: Intentionally or unintentionally winning a rally by smashing a ball into the body of a defenseless player standing across the court at the non-volley-zone line. This is also sometimes called a "body bag."

Used in a sentence: "I've got a bruise on my arm from a meat volley in yesterday's game."

***

N is for "Nasty Nelson"

Definition: A serve that intentionally hits the non-receiving opponent as he or she is standing near the non-volley-zone line and not expecting the ball.

Under the rules of pickleball, if either player on the other side is hit by the ball, the serving team wins the point.

Used in a sentence: "I think you have to be pretty desperate to try to win a point with a Nasty Nelson."

***

O is for "open play"

Definition: When pickleball courts use open play, it means that courts can't be reserved, but are instead used by players on a rotating basis. When a group of players finish a game, the court is yielded to the next group of four players waiting to play.

Players typically reserve their spots in line by putting their paddles in a rack. Players who relinquish the court can then play again by putting their paddles at the end of the waiting line of paddles.

Used in a sentence: "The problem with open play is that I usually end up with one or more players who are either way better than me or just learning how to play."

***

P is for "play it again"

Definition: Even though pickleball rules frown on do-overs as a way to resolve questioned line calls, some players find it's always worth a try.

Used in a sentence: "Yeah, I didn't get a great look. We could just play it again."

***

Q is for "quiet balls"

Definition: Due to complaining residents living near pickleball courts, some players have been forced to play with quiet balls, such as the Gamma Foam Quiet Ball

Used in a sentence: "The quiet ball is lighter and it bounces differently from traditional pickleballs, but if it's the only way we can play, it will have to do."

***

R is for "rally"

Definition: The back and forth action following the serve.

Used in a sentence: "There's nothing more fun in pickleball than a long rally that ends with a bold, decisive shot."

***

S is for "Shake & Bake"

Definition: The "shake and bake" is an aggressive offensive strategy that involves one partner hitting a low-and-hard drive (as an alternative to a drop shot) while his or her partner crashes the net, looking for a putaway from a weak, pop-up return.

Used in a sentence: "They were expecting a third-shot drop when we caught them by surprise by trying the Shake & Bake."

***

T is for "tennis shot"

Definition: A derogatory term used by pickleball players to describe a shot by an opponent that has a lot of windup or wrist action in its delivery.

It's a term usually used when that shot is delivered successfully.

Used in a sentence: "Nice tennis shot, Herb. You know, if it wasn't for the wind, that shot woulda' been long."

***

U is for "underhand"

Definition: An underhand serve in pickleball means that the ball must be struck below the waist, which is defined as the navel, and that the highest point of the paddle must be below the wrist when the ball is hit.

Used in a sentence: "One of the best things about pickleball is that underhand serves make for fewer aces and longer rallies."

***

V is for "volley llama"

Definition: Hitting a volley in the non-volley zone resulting in a fault.

Used in a sentence: "If you don't pay attention to your foot position, you could end up ruining a good rally with a volley llama."

***

W is for "wind"

Definition: The all-purpose excuse for all falafels and other poorly executed, unforced errors and errant balls you hit while playing outdoors.

Used in a sentence: "I was ready to hit a winner, and then there was this gust of wind at the last second."

***

X is for "X-rated language"

Definition: "Excessive profanity" — whatever that may be — is prohibited in the rules of pickleball. In tournament play it could result in a technical foul assessed by the referee, which would add a point to your opponent's score.

Used in a sentence: "No way was that @#$%#@#% ball out, you @#$%@#$% cheater."

***

Y is for "young people"

Definition: Anybody who moves faster than you on the court and doesn't talk about his or her sciatica during water breaks.

Used in a sentence: "Sometimes during open play a bunch of young people show up, making it hard to have a competitive game."

***

Z is for "zero-zero-two"

Definition: The doubles game starts at "zero-zero-two", which means that both sides have no points and the serving team starts with its second server.

Used in a sentence: "Patiently explaining to a newbie why the game begins at zero-zero-two is the price we have to pay for pickleball evangelism."